German American
Ach

400 Years of Contributions to America

DON HEINRICH TOLZMANN

Heritage Books. Inc.

Other Heritage Books publications by the author:

CD-ROMs:
German-American Biographical Index (CD-ROM)
The German Colonial Era (CD-ROM)
HB Archives: Germans Vol. 2 (CD-ROM)

Books:
German Pioneers in Early California: Erwin G. Gudde's History
AMANA: William Rufus Perkins' and Barthinius L. Wick's History of
The Amana Society or Community of True Inspiration
Pennsylvania Germans: James Owen Knauss, Jr.'s Social History
Kentucky's German Pioneers: H.A. Rattermann's History
Covington's (KY) German Heritage

German Allied Troops in the American Revolution:
J.R. Rosengarten's Survey of German Archives and Sources

German-Americana: A Bibliography

German Immigration in America: The First Wave

Memories of the Battle of New Ulm: Personal Accounts of the Sioux
Uprising. L.A. Fritsche's History of Brown County, Minnesota

Published 2001 by
HERITAGE BOOKS, INC.
Publishing Division
65 East Main Street
Westminster, Maryland 21157-5026
1-800-398-7709 / www.HeritageBooks.com

ISBN 0-7884-1993-5
A Complete Catalog Listing Hundreds of Titles
On History, Genealogy, and Americana
Available Free Upon Request

Table of Contents

Preface vii

I. Immigration and Settlement 1

   1. Introduction 5

   2. German Immigration 9

   3. The Age of Discovery 15

   4. Jamestown 17

   5. Germantown 21

   6. German Settlements Before the Revolution 23

   7. The German-American Farmer 29

   8. Settlement Patterns 33

II. Preserving the Union 35

   9. Germans in the Revolutionary War 39

  10. In the Civil War 45

  11. Service in Other Wars 49

III. Building the Nation 51

  12. Industrial Influences 55

  13. Social Influences 63

  14. Educational Influences 67

  15. Musical Influences 73

  16. Artistic Influences 77

  17. Film Influences 81

  18. Political Influences 83

  19. Journalistic Influences 89

  20. Literary Influences 93

  21. Linguistic Influences 97

  22. Religious Influences 105

IV: The German-American Experience 109

  23. The German-American Heritage 113

  24. Coming to America 115

  25. Home Away From Home 117

26. The Anti-German Hysteria 119
27. A Revival of Ethnic Pride 121
28. German-Americans Today 127
V. Appendix: The German American Heritage Month 131
VI. Select Bibliography 139
About the Author 145
Index 147

.

Was du ererbt von deinen Vätern hast
Erwirb es um es zu besitzen!

What your forebears bequeathed unto you,
Earn it anew to make it truly your own!

Goethe

Preface

This work aims to provide a concise survey of the role that America's largest ethnic group, the German-Americans, has played in American history, from the 17th century to the present. German-American history is, of course, too complex and multi-dimensional a topic to cover in a brief survey, but the basic outlines and essential characteristics clearly stand forth and are presented here for the purpose of a general overview. In preparing this work, I have especially drawn on my book, *The German-American Experience*, to which readers are referred for more comprehensive coverage. Those interested in further information are referred to the bibliography for a selection of works on various aspects of German-American history.

The motivation for putting this work together was the large number of requests I have often received for a brief survey, which would illuminate the outlines of German-American history, as well as identify the major influences German-Americans have exerted in the building of the nation.

At the very outset, it should be noted that the term "German-American" is used to refer to immigrants and their offspring from Germany, Austria, Switzerland, and other German-speaking areas of Europe. Hence, the term "German" is used here in a linguistic, cultural, and ethnic sense to cover the totality of the German-speaking immigrants and their descendants.

This work is divided into six parts. Part I, "Immigration and Settlement" traces German-American history from the earliest beginnings into the present time, while Parts II and III demonstrate the role German-Americans have played in terms of "Preserving the Union" and in "Building the Nation." In Part IV, "the German-American Experience" aims to provide an overview of the totality of the German-American experience. Part V consists of an Appendix regarding the annual German-American Heritage Month. Finally, in

Part VI is a "Select Bibliography," which is followed by the "Index." Special thanks to Robert E. Ward, Baldwin-Wallace College, for his translation of the poem by Konrad Krez used in this volume. Also, many thanks to Dorothy Young, Editorial Assistant for the German-American Studies Program at the University of Cincinnati for the final preparation of the manuscript of this work. Finally, this Preface is followed by a map and Census statistics from a volume by Gerard Wilk, edited by the author, which is referenced in the bibliography of selected works.

Don Heinrich Tolzmann

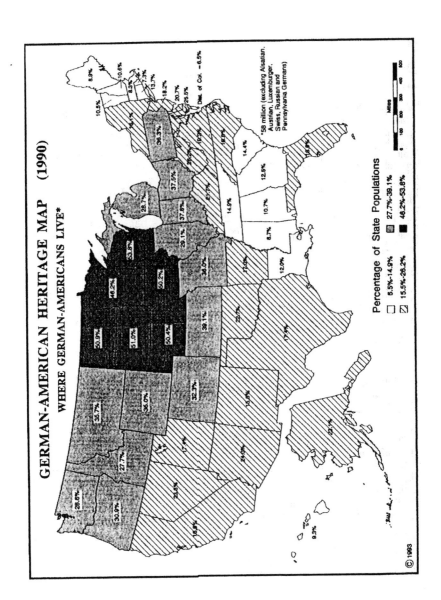

German-American Census Statistics

States	Total Population	German Pop.	% by State	% of Total
California	29,760,021	4,935,147	16.58%	1.98%
Pennsylvania	11,881,643	4,314,762	36.31%	1.73%
Ohio	10,847,115	4,067,840	37.50%	1.64%
Illinois	11,430,602	3,326,248	29.10%	1.34%
Texas	16,986,510	2,949,686	17.36%	1.19%
New York	17,990,455	2,898,888	16.11%	1.17%
Michigan	9,295,297	2,666,179	28.68%	1.07%
Wisconsin	4,891,769	2,630,680	53.78%	1.06%
Florida	12,937,926	2,410,257	18.63%	0.97%
Indiana	5,544,159	2,084,667	37.60%	0.84%
Minnesota	4,375,099	2,020,975	46.19%	0.81%
Missouri	5,117,073	1,843,299	36.02%	0.74%
New Jersey	7,730,188	1,407,956	18.21%	0.57%
Iowa	2,776,755	1,394,542	50.22%	0.56%
Washington	4,866,692	1,009,914	28.56%	0.56%
Maryland	4,781,468	1,218,257	25.48%	0.49%
Virginia	6,187,358	1,186,056	19.17%	0.48%
North Carolina	6,628,637	1,110,581	16.75%	0.45%
Colorado	3,294,394	1,063,694	32.29%	0.43%
Kansas	2,477,574	968,078	39.07%	0.39%
Oregon	2,842,321	878,555	30.91%	0.35%
Arizona	3,665,228	878,088	23.96%	0.35%
Georgia	6,478,216	810,165	12.51%	0.33%
Kentucky	3,685,296	798,001	21.65%	0.32%
Nebraska	1,578,385	794,911	50.36%	0.32%
Tennessee	4,877,185	724,059	14.85%	0.29%
Oklahoma	3,145,585	714,184	22.70%	0.29%
Louisiana	4,219,973	507,453	12.03%	0.20%
South Carolina	3,486,703	500,089	14.34%	0.20%
Massachusetts	6,016,425	497,462	8.27%	0.20%
West Virginia	1,793,477	468,927	26.15%	0.19%
Connecticut	3,287,116	450,247	13.70%	0.18%
Alabama	4,040,587	430,442	10.65%	0.17%
Arkansas	2,350,725	400,234	17.03%	0.16%
South Dakota	696,004	355,102	51.02%	0.14%
North Dakota	638,800	324,923	50.87%	0.13%
Utah	1,722,850	299,414	17.38%	0.12%
Montana	799,065	285,385	35.71%	0.11%
Nevada	1,201,833	279,693	23.27%	0.11%
Idaho	1,006,749	278,615	27.67%	0.11%
New Mexico	1,515,069	234,000	15.44%	0.09%
Mississippi	2,573,216	224,674	8.73%	0.09%
Wyoming	453,588	158,469	34.94%	0.06%
Delaware	666,168	138,128	20.73%	0.06%
Alaska	550,043	127,103	23.11%	0.05%
New Hampshire	1,109,252	118,003	10.64%	0.05%
Maine	1,227,928	108,859	8.87%	0.04%
Hawaii	1,108,229	102,714	9.27%	0.04%
Rhode Island	1,003,464	73,425	7.32%	0.03%
Vermont	562,758	59,090	10.50%	0.02%
District of Columbia	606,900	39,218	6.46%	0.02%
Total Statistics U. S. A.	248,709,873	57,947,338	23.30%	23.30%

I. Immigration and Settlement

Da waren Deutsche auch dabei!

Als Bettler sind wir nicht gekommen
Aus unserem deutschen Vaterland.
Wir hatten manches mitgenommen,
Was hier noch fremd und unbekannt
Und als man schuf aus dichten Wäldern,
Aus öder, düstrer Wüstenei
Den Kranz von reichen Feldern,
Da waren Deutsche auch dabei.

At Your Side, There Were Germans, Too!

Not as burdens to these shores we throng,
From our cherished German Fatherland.
Indeed, we have brought so much along,
Unknown to you, yet by our hand.
And when from the dense forestal shields,
And the open wilderness you
Wreath'd your vast and verdant fields,
At your side there were Germans too.

Konrad Krez

1. Introduction

The history of the German-Americans goes back to the earliest colonial period, to the very beginnings of American history, when the first permanent German settlers arrived at Jamestown on 1 October 1608. Recurrent waves in the colonial period were followed by great tides of German immigration in the 19ᵗʰ and 20ᵗʰ centuries and these carried into the population of the United States an element which is now the largest ethnic stock in the country. According to the U.S. Census, some sixty million report German ancestry.

Given the sheer size of the German element, it is not altogether surprising that it is essential to understand the history of German immigration and settlement, as well as the role German-Americans have played in the growth and development of the country. As German-Americans are the largest ethnic group in the U.S., and the predominant group in 23 states of the Union, this is especially true for an understanding of state and local history.

Indeed, it is no understatement, but rather a simple fact, that if you do not understand the role German-Americans have played in the history and development of the U.S., then you cannot really fathom and understand American history. Another way to put it, is that any history which does not include, or provide proportional coverage of one-fourth of the nation's population is clearly incorrect and incomplete.

Although German-Americans constitute the largest ethnic element in the U. S., their history has remained relatively obscured until the recent past. Indeed, it might be observed that the largest ethnic group in the U.S. has received the least amount of coverage in the standard works of American history. Often there is little, or no mention made of German-Americans.

Moreover, when prominent German-Americans, such as von Steuben, Schurz, and von Braun, are mentioned, they are rarely identified as such. The absence of German-Americans and the role they have played in American history, as well as the reticence regarding this role in the standard works of American history is readily apparent, especially to those of German descent.

The fact that German-Americans have been largely excluded, ignored, and overlooked for much of the twentieth century is a direct result of two factors. First, up until the recent past, the role ethnic groups have played in American history has been for the most part overlooked and neglected by an Anglo-centric historiography influenced by the "melting pot" concept. This caused ethnic groups to record their own histories and often in their own languages. These were then usually belittled as being "filiopietistic," and thus readily ignored.

However, from the point of view of the various ethnic groups, mainstream history was by and large Anglo-filiopietistic. Had they not taken on the tasks of recording their own history, no one else would have risen to the task. Also, it should be noted that, early on, German-American history was written predominantly in the German language and was thus inaccessible to those not conversant in German. Hence, historiographically and linguistically, German-Americans were not on the agenda with regard to the writing of American history.

A second factor, and one which has affected German-Americans alone, was the anti-German hysteria and sentiment of the two world wars. This tended to obscure the role German-Americans have played in American history. Only recently has there been an upswing of interest in according German-Americans their appropriate place in the annals of American history.

In the 1950s, German-American organizations actively resumed their program of activities, at the same time as German-American relations became a focal point of the NATO alliance. However, it was not really until the ethnic revival of the 1970s, particularly after the celebration of the American Bicentennial in 1976, and beyond that there was again wide scale public recognition and pride in the German heritage.

With this recognition and pride has come the interest as well as the need to learn more about the history of the German-Americans. The challenge, therefore, is to illuminate and make known the role played by German-Americans in American history. Before we review their history, however, we first need to broadly trace the history of the causes and reasons for the German immigrations.

2. German Immigration

Historically, there have been three periods in the history of German immigration: first, before 1820; second, from 1820 to 1920; and, finally, since 1920. About 85% of the German-speaking immigrants came from Germany, while the other 15% came from other German-speaking countries and areas of Europe, such as Austria, Bohemia, Moravia, Liechtenstein, Switzerland, Alsace-Lorraine, certain parts of Russia, Yugoslavia, Hungary, Romania, Poland.

The causes of the immigration were numerous and complex. Many came for religious and political reasons, or to avoid military service. However, economic conditions were the predominant factors. Much more significant for the millions was the prospect of making a better living in the New World. In immigration history, we speak of the push and pull factors, which cause individuals to be moved to leave their homelands and to be drawn to new ones. In the history of the German immigration there were numerous push and pull factors.

German Immigration Before 1820

Push factors:

1. The social, political, and economic conditions in the German states were decidedly negative, and had been so for centuries. In the 15th century, the plague, or black death, had laid waste to at least 25% of the population. In the 16th century, religious strife and warfare swept across Germany, which left it divided confessionally and politically. In the 17th century, the 30 Years War (1618-48) raged across Europe, which resulted in the loss for the second time of 25% of the population of Germany. Hence, by the time the

immigration got underway, Germany was a shattered, war-torn land without a viable central government.

2. Second, was the factor of German disunity. Although the German states were theoretically held together by the institution called Holy Roman Empire of the German Nation, in practice the hallmark of this empire was disunity. The numerous principalities were virtually autonomous states with Prussia and Austria emerging as the superpowers. Real authority now resided with the individual states. The absence of a strong central government meant that there was no such thing as a national economy and, of course, no national defense and security. This made the German states relatively easy prey for French aggression from the century and half after the Thirty Years War to the age of Napoleon.

Pull factors:

1. First, there was a basic land hunger amongst prospective immigrants. This was due to the fact that in the southwest German states the land was equally subdivided amongst all the children, with the result that individual farms were becoming much too small to be commercially stable with each generation. Northeastern Germany had another inheritance. Here the land passed on to the eldest son, which meant that all the other children had to look elsewhere for their future means of support. America, obviously, would appear like a beacon of hope to many in Europe, particularly in the German states.

2. There was extensive literature about America, which was called *Amerika-Literatur*. It painted a vivid picture of the numerous positive possibilities for a new existence in America, which contrasted sharply with the harsh socio-economic, and political realities of the conditions in the German states

3. Companies or societies would be established which would plan and organize immigration and settlement in America, such as

the Frankfurt Company, which would organize the settlement of Germantown, Pennsylvania.

4. Immigration to certain areas in America would establish contacts between the old and new worlds. Thousands and eventually millions of letters by immigrants writing home motivated others to follow, thus establishing what became known as "chain migration" between the Old and New Worlds.

German Immigration from 1820 to 1920

Push factors:

1. First, there was a great deal of disillusionment and dissatisfaction with the condition in the German Federation period after the Napoleonic wars. It should be noted that France had waged war on the continent from 1792 down through the era of the French emperor, and that Germans had fought enthusiastically to bring about the downfall of the dictator in the hopes that there would be substantive political reform toward national unity and political freedom. When under the leadership of Prince Metternich of Austria the authoritarianism and autocracy of the German princes was re-established, there was a great deal of bitterness and resentment.

2. Second, in 1815-16, the German states were struck with disastrous crop failures and excessively harsh winters, causing great hardships in rural areas, which in turn impacted on urban populations.

3. Third, there were a number of protests and revolutions in 1817, 1832, and 1848, which caused Germans to leave their homelands. The major objective in these political undertakings was the establishment of German unity within the framework of a constitutional monarchy, or republican form of government.

4. A fourth factor was military conscription and the desire to escape the long history of warfare in Europe. Located in the center of an area without natural boundaries, the German states were

required to maintain standing armies for security purposes. Even so, due to its geographical location, many of the major battles in European history were fought in central Europe, such as the Battle of Nations, which was fought at Leipzig and finally brought about the downfall of Napoleon.

5. Fifth, in the late 19th century socialists left Germany because of the anti-socialists legislation promulgated by the chancellor of Germany, Otto von Bismarck.

6. Sixth, for religious reasons German Lutherans and Catholics left, the former in the early 19th and the latter in the late 19th century. German Lutherans left, as they objected to the merger of the Reformed and Lutheran Churches, which the King of Prussia had ordered. German Catholics left because of the anti-Catholic program of Bismarck known as the *Kulturkampf*.

7. Finally, among the economic reasons was the continued land hunger of prospective immigrants as well as the decline of small crafts and trades as a result of the industrial revolution, both of which caused individuals to look towards America in the hope of a better future.

Pull factors:

1. First, chain migration was now well established, and sending continual series of immigrants to the New World.

2. Second, there were further attempts at organized immigration by means of plans to establish German-American states in Wisconsin, Missouri, and Texas.

3. Third, the literature about America continued to be published, and by the mid-19th century the image of America had achieved the status of the El Dorado of the German immigrant.

4. Finally, a major pull factor was the Homestead Act of 1862, which lasted until 1892, and meant that the immigrant could obtain

160 acres of public land cost-free, if one would improve the land, and reside on it for a minimum of five years.

German immigration since 1920

Push factors:

1. First, with the conclusion of the First World War came the unfortunate dissolution of the centuries-old empires, the German and the Austro-Hungarian Empire. This general loss of social, economic, and political stability in central Europe led to increased immigration. Specifically, the loss of territories in eastern and southeastern Europe caused Germans in these areas, known as the Danube Swabians, to emigrate, as did the disastrous inflation of the 1920s.

2. Before and after the Second World War, hundreds of thousands emigrated to escape the tragic calamities of that period. This included increased numbers Danube Swabians to come to America. Many sought exile before the war because of their opposition to and/or persecution by the Third Reich, whereas millions were driven from their ancestral homelands in eastern and southeastern Europe after the war.

Two groups of immigrants often overlooked were, first, the 300,000 "war brides" who married American G.I.s and then came to the U.S. in the 1950s, and second, the 5,000 former German P.O.W.s who decided to migrate to America after the war. In the Cold War period, numerous refugees made their way to the U.S. from behind the Iron Curtain.

Pull Factors:

1. First, the positive image of America was still being vividly portrayed in the literature dealing with the U.S., although this literature became increasingly critical as to the realities of immigrating and re-establishing oneself in the New World.

2. Second, the process of chain migration continued to send immigrants to America. Often, immigrants who came before and

after the wars, were in contact with friends, family, and relatives who had immigrated earlier to the U.S.

Results:

The result of this century-long history of German immigration is that more than eight million German-speaking immigrants came to America, and that there are now more than sixty million German-Americans. Geographically, most German-Americans are located in what has been called the "German Belt," which refers to the states which stretch from Pennsylvania in the east through the middle west and great plains states all the way to the west coast. In all of these states, Americans of German descent constitute the largest ethnic group.

3. The Age of Discovery

When America was discovered, Spain, France, and England, which became the principal colonial powers in its exploitation, had already developed as nation-states with political centralization under their kings. Germany, on the other hand, remained decentralized favoring the territorial princes. Lacking also a national fleet, Germany was excluded from colonizing the North American continent. Moreover, Germany was embroiled in the 1500s with internal affairs revolving around the Reformation and the ensuing wars of religion.

Nevertheless, Germans did make a contribution during this epoch. Martin Behaim, one of the inventors of the astrolabe, in 1491-92 constructed a globe, the oldest one known in existence, for his native city, Nürnberg. This still records the best of the world's geographical knowledge of that date, and proves Behaim's conviction about the spherical shape of the earth before the discovery of America.

And, there was Mercator (Gerhard Kramer), the inventor of the Mercator system of projection, taking account of the curvature of the earth's surface in the preparation of nautical maps, an indispensable aid to the early mariners, who sailed across the Atlantic to the New World.

It is said that there were a few Germans on board the voyage with Columbus in 1492, and that they were scholars knowledgeable of and conversant in Biblical and ancient languages, and that they were brought along to assist in the communication process with the inhabitants of the New World.

The person who first used the name "America" in a printed work was Martin Waldseemüller, born in Freiburg ca. 1480. In 1507, he published his Cosmographiae Introductio, in which he gives an account of the voyages of Amerigo Vespucci, and suggests that the new continent be named after him. The best maps and globes at this time were made by German cartographers and printers. They aided the navigation process and disseminated knowledge of the newly discovered lands.

The first expeditions to the New World centered on South America: In 1528, Karl V., Kaiser of the Holy Roman Empire of the German Nation, as well as King of Spain, had assigned the territory of Venezuela to the banking house of the Welsers of Nürnberg. They established the first colony there - 80 years before the colony at Plymouth, Massachusetts.

Nikolaus Federmann, Georg Hohermuth, and Ambrosius Dalfinger went on hazardous expeditions and penetrated the jungle as far as Bogata. From the 1560s onwards, there were a scattered number of Germans in various expeditions, which landed on the Atlantic coast of what is now the U.S., but none resulted in a permanent settlement. This would not be accomplished until the early years of the 17th century.

4. Jamestown

In all the earliest colonies along the Atlantic coast there were sporadic cases of German settlers, the first being at Jamestown, Virginia in 1608. These first permanent German settlers arrived on or around the 1st of October 1608, which is the actual beginning date of German-American history. They crossed the Atlantic on the good ship *Mary and Margaret*.

The 400th anniversary of the arrival of these first Germans will take place in 2008, at which time the German-American Quadricentennial will be celebrated in conjunction with the annual celebration of German-American Day on the 6th of October.

In 1997, a historic marker was erected at Jamestown with the following inscription:

> The first Germans to land at Jamestown in Virginia, arrived aboard the vessel *Mary and Margaret* about 1 October 1608. These Germans were glassmakers and carpenters. In 1620, German mineral specialists and saw-millwrights followed, to work and settle in the Virginia colony. These pioneers and skilled craftsmen were the forerunners of the many millions of Germans who settled in America and became the single largest national group to populate the Untied States.

Thereafter, Germans were especially to be found in New Amsterdam, later New York, and New Sweden, subsequently part of Pennsylvania. In the Dutch settlement of New Amsterdam, later New York, and New Sweden, subsequently part of Pennsylvania. In the Dutch settlement of New Amsterdam there were two German-American leaders second to none in shaping the destinies of the colonies: Peter Minuit, the founder and first governor of the colony,

Peter Minuit, born at Wesel-on-the-Rhine, was appointed governor of New Netherlands by the Dutch West India Co., and bought the island of Manhattan from the Indians in 1626. Under his leadership, the colony became the successful rival of New England in the remunerative fur trade. Shipbuilding was carried on, and in 1631, the *New Netherland* was launched, one of the largest ships afloat at the time. On his departure in 1632, Minuit left the colony in a most prosperous condition. In Holland the returning governor was, unfortunately, made the scapegoat for the evils of the Dutch patroon system. He left deeply mortified by this ingratitude of the Dutch West India Co., and offered his services to the ruler of Sweden.

The result was that he became for the second time the founder of an important colony. He arrived in Delaware Bay in April 1638, and built Fort Christina near the present site of Wilmington. New Sweden rapidly grew in trade and colonists, and for a long time preserved its independence. Minuit died at his post in 1641.

Not quite fifty years later, there lived another great German-American leader, Jacob Leisler, born in Frankfurt am Main, who appeared in New York in 1661. He was a trader, who amassed wealth through the boldness and genius of his ventures. Though allied by marriage with the Dutch aristocracy, he remained democratic at heart, and a representative of the middle-class people, who trusted his simple honesty, admired his rugged individualism, and honored his public spirit and liberality.

In 1689, when the news arrived of the landing of William of Orange in England, a popular revolt broke out in New York against the hated rule of the English Gov. Nicholson and his party. The revolution placed Leisler at the head and made him provisional governor. The administration of Leisler is truly memorable in colonial history because it was he who was the first to call together a congress of the American colonies for cooperative action.

In April 1690, Leisler invited the governors of Massachusetts, Plymouth, East and West Jersey, Pennsylvania, Maryland and Virginia to a common council in New York. This meeting of 1 May 1690, was the first congress of American colonies convened entirely by the colonists. Invasion by the French and Indians threatened from without, and England, in the throes of revolution, could not be relied on for aid.

In this congress, the first step toward cooperation and independence was taken in the history of the American colonies; this was the great forerunner of the American Continental Congress, and to Jacob Leisler belongs the honor of having convened it.

The subsequent triumph of Leisler's enemies resulted in the re-establishment of a reactionary government by Col. Sloughter. This led to the martyrdom of Leisler, who was executed with his son-in-law, Milborne, on the trumped-up charge of high treason. This tragic fate serves only to dignify the brilliant achievement of the first people's governor of New York.

It should be noted that in these early years, Germans were often referred to as the "Dutch." For example, Captain John Smith referred to them as Dutchmen, when he noted that they were instrumental in introducing the first sawmill, glass-blowing shops, and vineyards. The confusion of "Dutch" and "Deutsch" is readily understood given the similarity of the two terms. Also, Holland itself was still legally part of Germany until 1648. Moreover, many of the first Germans settled at the Dutch colony of New Amsterdam. In time, however, the distinction came to be made between the "High Dutch" for the Germans and the "Low Dutch" for the Hollanders. Today, though in popular usage, this contrastive pair refers more to speakers of the "Upper German" and "Low German" dialects.

5. Germantown

The close of the 17th century saw the establishment of the first permanent German settlement in America. This was Germantown, Pennsylvania, which was established in 1683, under the leadership of Franz Daniel Pastorius. The 6th of October was the date of the arrival of the good ship *Concord*, considered the *Mayflower* of the German immigration. Although Germans were present in the colonies prior to this date, they had been scattered throughout the settlements, whereas with Germantown, Germans had founded the first all-German settlement. Philadelphia had been founded but two years before this, and the liberal policy of William Penn attracted this small band of religious refugees to Penn's colony in the New World.

These German settlers were mostly Mennonite and Quakers from Krefeld, and weavers by trade. The scholar Pastorius was their guiding spirit, though his Latin books were not as good an equipment as the looms of the Krefelders. Farming and manufacturing became the occupations of the Germantown settlement and they remained so for generations to come.

A minimum of time was given to public life, as the most pressing concern was establishing oneself in the New World. Also, some objected to participation in public affairs on the basis of their religious fath. For example, Arnold Küster, the immigrant ancestor of Gen. George Armstrong Custer, was elected a committeeman of Germantown in 1702, but refused to serve because of conscientious objection based on his Mennonite faith. It, hence, became necessary to impose a fine for the refusal to accept public office for election.

However, Germantowners were ready to take a stand on issues of concern. They immortalized themselves by their protest against slavery in 1688, the first formal action ever taken against the barter in human flesh within the boundaries of what is today the U.S.

Another deed of imperishable fame was the printing of the German Lutheran Bible in the German language by Christoph Saur, of Germantown, in 1743, the first Bible printed in a European language in the American colonies.

Germantown itself would remain "the" German-American social, cultural, economic, and political center well into the early 19th century, and thereafter would continue to hold significant cultural importance. Rudolf Cronau wrote of Germantown: "What Plymouth Rock is to Anglo-Americans, Germantown is to Americans of German descent, a spot consecrated by history, a spot where every American should stand with uncovered head." Cronau's observation provides insight as to the importance of Germantown in German-American history.

6. German Settlements Before the Revolution

The great waves of German immigration began to rise in the second decade of the 18th century, and they flowed and ebbed alternately until the period of the Revolutionary War. Many refugees from religious persecution appeared, but the great bulk were induced to emigrate for political and economic reasons.

The "push" and "pull" factors of the German immigration are seen at work here. On the one side, poor conditions at home, sometimes aggravated to the point of separation, caused the "push" factor, and on the other side, better, or more favorable conditions, or at least the hope for improved conditions, provided the "pull" factors, thus causing Germans to come to America.

Favorable reports from colonists went back to Germany and whetted the appetite for emigration to such an extent that some home governments felt it necessary to confiscate favorable letters with the same eagerness as if they were emigrant agents. The region of Germany which during the 18th century furnished the greatest number of immigrants was the upper Rhine territory, going southward from the entry of the Main into the Rhine and extending into the mountains of Switzerland.

The Rhenish Palantinate, Southwestern Germany, and German Switzerland were sections suffering from crop failures, over-populations, and French aggression and warfare—causes which produced a continuous flow of immigration to what was then known as the West India Islands, the island of Pennsylvania and the island of Carolina figuring the most prominently in the popular imagination.   Where did they settle? Did they remain in the seaport towns? Rarely, or not long. Most of them were skilled cultivators of the soil, whose ambition it was to own land and build upon it a home of their own. If they were tradesmen, expert in some handicraft, they might remain longer in the seaport to practice their trade, but only long enough to enable them to save enough money to buy land. Where could land be bought cheaply and in sufficient quantity to make a farm pay?

The farms around the seaports and for some distance inland were very soon bought up by older settlers who had accumulated larger means and preferred the security of the seaboard area. The new colonists had to try their fortunes westward if they wished to secure land within their means. As a result of this, large number of English and Dutch settled on the seacoast, while the German, Irish, Scotch, and Hugenot settlers went to the frontier as pioneers.

Their colonies became buffers against the Indians, and thereby a protection for the coast settlements. It is most remarkable to see how largely the frontier settlements about the period of the Revolutionary War were inhabited by German and Irish immigrants, who had come without means. If we draw a frontier line for the year 1775 from outpost to outpost in the then westernmost sections we will find that the German settlers had a very large share in the defense of the frontier line during the 18th century.

Even at the extremities of the line in Maine and Georgia there were German settlers. In Maine, at Waldoboro, a German colony was established in 1742 on Broad Bay; in Georgia there existed prosperous settlements of the Salzburgers. These German Lutherans, a portion of those exiled in 1731 by the fanatical zeal of Archbishop Leopold, came to Georgia under the auspices of General Oglethorpe in 1734, the year after he had founded Savannah.

The Salzburgers had excellent leaders in their preachers, Bolzius and Gronau, and in Baron von Reck, who laid out the first settlement at Ebenezer. Numerous were the settlement of the Salzburgers in the district of the Savannah River, which at that time was the only inhabited portion of Georgia.

Following the frontier in 1775, we find that the farthermost westward colonists in New York were the German settlers in the Mohawk Valley, a section which was exposed as no other pioneer territory to the incursions of the most warlike Indian tribes, the Six Nations.

The German settlers of Schoharie had their share of the burden to bear, being also exposed on their western border. In Pennsylvania, we find that the midland and southwestern sections were occupied by German settlers, who made this territory famous for agricultural wealth.

At the time of the Revolution, they numbered one-third of the population of the Commonwealth of Pennsylvania. From Lancaster County they crossed the Susquehanna River, settled York and Adams counties, then they trekked southward, following the base of the mountains and settled Frederick County, Maryland.

In Maryland, they also went westward into Washington and eastward into Carroll County. They went still farther southward, crossed the Cumberland River and followed the Shenandoah up through the Valley of Virginia. The Shenandoah Valley, as far as Augusta County became as German as Lancaster County, Pennsylvania, and was its rival in agricultural prosperity.

The Valley of Virginia became the great avenue to the New Southwest. The southern slope of the Shenandoah Valley was occupied more largely by Irish settlers, but in the course of time Germans also settled there and took part in the settlement of Kentucky and Tennessee as soon as the gateways were opened by the Indian wars during and following the Revolution.

In North Carolina, the westerly counties then on the frontier along the Yadkin and Catawba Rivers were inhabited by Germans and Irish as neighbors in nearly equal numbers. The Germans had come all the way from Pennsylvania. It was the custom to harvest a summer crop and sell it along with the farm, to load one's possessions on a big wagon and start out with a family and cattle in the fall of the year.

Autumn and winter months were devoted entirely to the long trip from Pennsylvania to Maryland, then up to the Shenandoah Valley and down part way on the other side to the headwaters of one or other of the Virginia rivers, which would open the way toward North Carolina. The example given by the German Moravians, who about 1750 settled a large tract in the Wachovia district of North Carolina, in what is now Forsyth and Stokes Counties. This settlement, Winston-Salem, still exists and is one of the most quaint and prosperous agricultural districts in the Carolinas.

In South Carolina, the settlement of the western areas was not made from the north, but from the seacoast, from the seaport Charleston, which was important for the German immigration to the southeast. There was in South Carolina, a promised land for German settlers just as there had been in New York State. Tradition had it that the generous Queen Anne had set aside Schoharie County in New York for the thousands of Palatines who had come to England in 1710, pleading to be sent as colonists to the American settlements. Similarly Queen Anne was said to have designated the then western section of South Carolina for settlement by the Palatines.

Whether there was any truth in the traditions or not, it is a well established fact that the bulk of the early settlers in the Saxe-Gotha district, then the western, now the central, section of South Carolina, were German immigrants who settled there from 1735 onwards. The records of fifteen protestant churches, most of them German Lutheran, several German Reformed, furnish conclusive evidence of the massing of German settlers in Saxe-Gotha, at present the counties of Orangeburg and Lexington in South Carolina.

While the preceding show the considerable share of the German element in the defense and advance of the frontier in the 18th century, it must not be forgotten that the Germans also left an impress on other areas.

They had distinctive German settlements on the coast line, such as Waldoboro in Maine, Newburgh in New York, New Bern in North Carolina, Germantown near Philadelphia, and a strong nucleus of settlers in the seaport cities of New York, Philadelphia, Baltimore, and Charleston.

7. The German-American Farmer

A great value of German immigrants was their service as farmers in the midland area. No one has expressed greater appreciation of this fact than Dr. Benjamin Rush, a most eminent American physician of his time and a signer of the Declaration of Independence. In an essay on the manners and customs of the Pennsylvania Germans (1789), he points out the particular virtues of the German farmer in America.

Rush demonstrates that they were experts in their occupation; that they were industrious and economical; that they knew good land when they saw it and kept possession of it when they obtained it; that they rotated their crops, took good care of their stock and were not afraid of hard work. Dr. Rush emphasizes the importance of their success in the economic foundations of the Commonwealth of Pennsylvania. He said it made possible the establishment and successful operation of the Bank of North America, the original financial backbone of the nation.

Similarly, the German immigrants of the 19th century have kept alive the good reputation of the German farmer in the U.S. At three basic points they pushed the frontier line westward - in Wisconsin, Missouri, and Texas. The entire Midwest also received a large share of the German immigrants of the 19th century, these in addition to the descendants of the 18th century settlers who migrated westward from Pennsylvania, the Virginias, Maryland, and Carolinas.

Statistics show that the English and Scandinavian farmers were also prosperous and skillful. The Germans, however, for a period of more than two centuries have consistently maintained the reputation of being the most successful farmers in the U.S.

Upon the industrious and conscientious work of the German small farmer depends in very large measure the wealth of the great

Midwest, the bread basket of the land. The great grain crops of the country, year after year, form the backbone of American financial prosperity. As in the past, German-Americans remain the largest single ethnic group in the field of agriculture.

Studies of agriculture in the Midwest, which compared German-American farmers with those of Yankee, or Anglo-American stock, came to the following conclusions. It was found that Yankee farmers were motivated more by the idea of becoming financially secure, while German-American Farmers were more interested in re-creating the kinds of close-knit farming communities they had left in Germany.

German-American farmers were more intent on farming such communities, whereas Yankees were not, as they did not have this sense of community.

Moreover, German-American farmers were not particularly interested in establishing bigger farms and were less likely to go into debt. They seemed to operate with a definite ceiling in mind as to how much they wanted to spend, and how large they wanted to expand their farms. For them, the main thing was to have enough land for their children and family. On the other hand, Yankee farmers were more motivated towards expansion, investment, and bigger and better farms, as their central goal was not directed at the family unit and the community.

Also, with German heritage farms there is the tendency to turn the farm over to the children, and then live nearby, whereas the Yankees tend to postpone retirement, and then are more likely to retire to Florida or Arizona.

The end result is that land ownership is high amongst farmers of German-American stock, and that there is an emphasis on community and family.

The importance of the German-American farmer is clearly underscored by the U.S. Census. According to the Census, 36% of the rural farm population of the country is German-American. In the twelve states of the Midwest, the percentage is even higher - 49%. American agriculture, therefore, is an area where German-Americans have exerted great influence.

8. Settlement Patterns

By 1900, German-Americans could be found settled throughout the U.S., but as a result of settlement patterns they showed a preponderance in the northern states, especially in the Midwest. The primary factors contributing to this regional concentration were, of course, chain-migration, climatic preference, and the absence of slavery.

If a line were drawn from Jamestown, Virginia westwards and connect with the Ohio River through to St. Louis and from there further with the Missouri River and onwards west, then the territory to the north would be fairly well delineated as the region, which became known as the German Belt.

German-speaking immigrants tended to gravitate to the states in this German Belt. They settled not only in the rural areas, but in the cities and towns as well. In the course of the 19th century the major urban German-American centers arose in Cincinnati, St. Louis, and Milwaukee, which became known as the famed "German Triangle."

Initially, many urban areas developed German districts, but as immigration increased in the course of the 19th century, the population of towns and cities in the Midwest often rose to be substantially or predominantly German in terms of ethnic origin. Hence, rather than speaking about German districts, percentages have to be cited with regard to urban areas, such as Cincinnati which became 58% of German stock by the 1890s. Some small towns rose to more than 80-90% German by the turn of the century.

Studying and being aware of the German heritage of the states of the German Belt is basic to an understanding of these areas and their social, cultural, economic, and political history.

II. Preserving the Union

Und wie in Bürgerkriegstagen,
Ja schon beim ersten Freiheitsschrei:
Wir dürfen's unbestritten sagen,
Da waren Deutsche auch dabei.

***

And so we declare in Lincoln's day,
And that day freedom's horn first blew -
Yes, we dare undeniably say:
At your side there were Germans too!

Konrad Krez

9. Germans in the Revolutionary War

A remarkable feature about German-Americans is that they have consistently served in numbers greater than their percentage of the population. This has been true from the 18th century to the present time.

At the very opening of the Revolutionary War, a German regiment was formed by vote of the Continental Congress in 1776. It was recruited in Pennsylvania and Maryland, and distinguished itself in the New Jersey campaign and in Sullivan's expedition against the Indians.

Of course, there were other German-American military units in the Revolution. Nicholas von Ottendorff's troops and John Paul Schott's dragoons performed valiant service as Armand's Legion, which was a corps of light cavalry. Von Heer's Independent Troop of the Horse provided personal bodyguard service to Washington, and holds distinction in the fact that Washington had a German-American bodyguard unit. This unit was also the last U. S. Army unit mustered out of service, as it accompanied Washington to his home at the end of the Revolution.

The best strategist after Washington, General Greene, had under him two reliable German-American brigadier generals: Peter Mühlenberg and Gerhard von der Wieden, whose regiments were composed mainly of Germans from the Valley of Virginia and elsewhere.

At Brandywine, Mühlenberg's brigade was used by General Greene in his daring maneuver that covered the retreat of the American army and prevented its annihilation by Cornwallis. At Germantown, Mühlenberg's brilliant bayonet attack pierced the enemy's right wing.

Peter Mühlenberg, was the son of the founder of the German Lutheran Church in America, and brother of Frederick Augustus Mühlenberg, the first speaker of the House of Representatives. After the Revolution, Mühlenberg was elected to the U.S. Senate, representing the state of Pennsylvania.

The fighting general, Baron Johann de Kalb sacrificed his life in the battle of Camden, heroically stemming the tide of defeat brought on by General Gates' blunders. In 1825 in Camden, Lafayette had a memorial built in honor of de Kalb whose inscriptions reads "German by birth, cosmopolitan by principle, his love of freedom made him help the citizens of the New World in their fight for independence."

It is not commonly known, but one third of the French troops sent to America to aid Americans in the American Revolution were German. This was due to the fact that France held possession of the German-speaking provinces of Alsace-Lorraine, which it had conquered in the 17th century. A cousin of General de Kalb was in the regiment of Prinz Wilhelm of Zweibrücken, one of several German regiments included in the French auxiliary forces at Yorktown. Captain Heinrich de Kalb was the first to enter the redoubt in the storming of one of the two forts which closed the siege of Yorktown, forcing the enemy to capitulate.

In the North, General Nicholas Herkimer, originally Herchheimer, led the German farmers of the Mohawk Valley against the invading army of St. Leger, and in the battle of Oriskany, in which he was mortally wounded, won the victory which cut off Burgoyne from supplies and relief from the west.

Reference should also be made to Christopher Ludwig, the German baker from Philadelphia, whom Congress appointed Superintendent of Baking for the entire army. He was an original anti-grafter, and Washington's "honest friend." One hundred pounds of bread were asked of him for every hundred pounds of flour. "No," said he, "Christopher Ludwig does not wish to become rich by the war. He has enough. Out of one hundred pounds of flour one gets one hundred and thirty-five pounds of bread, and so many will I give." All his predecessors had taken advantage of the ignorance of the legislators, who did not know that the added water increases the weight considerably.

Above all there clearly stands one German-American soldier, who takes place immediately after Washington and Greene in terms of service to the patriotic cause: General Friedrich Wilhelm von Steuben, the Inspector-General of the Continental Army. It is no exaggeration to say, that without the discipline and economy, without the knowledge of the elements of drill, maneuvering and campaigning which von Steuben infused into the militia, American independence could not have been won at that time.

Von Steuben, a veteran of the Seven Years War, a favorite pupil of Frederick the Great, the foremost general of the age, brought over the principles of Prussian military science and applied them to American conditions.

At Valley Forge the Inspector-General prepared the way for future victories, and in Virginia he recruited and drilled the forces that decided the southern campaign.

After the war, von Steuben remained in America, whose freedom he had helped to win, and identified himself with all its military interests, the founding of West Point, the fortification of New York City, the writing and rewriting of the *Regulations for the Order and Discipline of the Troops of the United States*, commonly referred to as *Von Steuben's Manual*, which remained the guide for American military discipline for more than a generation. Also, it should be noted that this work continues to be reprinted to the present day.

Also, it should be noted that Heinrich Lutterloh was appointed Quartermaster-General of the Continental Army in 1781. Thus, the three most important positions in the American forces were occupied by German-Americans: Inspector-General (von Steuben), Superintendent of Baking (Ludwig), and Quartermaster-General (Lutterloh). American troops were, therefore, trained, fed, and led by German-American officers.

Another point to be made in conclusion to a discussion of the role played by German-Americans in the American Revolution: they established the foundations of a record of outstanding military service above and beyond their percentage of population, a fact generally unknown and unreflected in the standard works of American history.

The names of more than 2,000 German-American soldiers, who fought in the American Revolution can be found listed in a work edited by the author, *German-Americans in the American Revolution: Henry Melchior Muhlenberg Richards' History* (1992). It should be remembered that no more than 18,000 American soldiers were in service at any given time, thus providing an indication of how important the German-American troops were.

A thorough search of the regimental listings of Pennsylvania, Maryland, Virginia, and New York, would of course, yield even more names, thus leading to the conclusion that German-Americans most likely formed a substantial percentage of the American forces in the American Revolution, although they constituted only ca. 10% of the population. In Pennsylvania, where Germans amounted to one-third of the population, their role was especially important for the following reason. The best estimate, based on an examination of regimental listings, would be that German-Americans numbered ca. one-fourth of the Continental Army.

Both they and the Anglo-Americans each constituted one-third of the population. However, it was estimated that one-third of the Anglo-Americans supported the Revolution, one-third were pro-British, and one-third were neutral. In the case of the Germans, it is estimated that perhaps as much as 90 percent supported the Revolution.

According to Rudolf Cronau's *German Achievements in America,* "The independence of the United States would probably not have been attained without the patriotic support" of the German element. Their participation was, hence, not only crucial, but essential for the final outcome of victory.

10. In the Civil War

Roughly one-third, or an estimated 800,000 of the 2.5 million soldiers in the Union Army in the Civil War were German-American, i.e. German-born, or of German stock. The German-born alone exceeded 200,000 (the Irish-born numbered 144,000 and the English-born 46,000). In terms of Union officers, it should be noted that 500 were German-born.

German-Americans, therefore, formed the backbone of the Union Army. Many German-Americans, it should be noted, had served in the Prussian Army, the best army in Europe, while many others had military experience by means of participation in the 1848 Revolution. This background would serve the Union well due to the fact that German-Americans formed the major single ethnic element in the Union Army.

In states, where German-Americans formed the predominant ethnic element, they served well beyond their percentage of the population. For example, Pennsylvania provided a sum total of 271,500 soldiers for the Union Army, of which 43% were German-American (17,208 German-
born and 100,000 of German stock).

Nine of the German-born officers attained the rank of major-general: Osterhaus, Sigel, Schurz, Willich, Steinwehr, Weitzel, Stahel, Kautz, and Salomon. A few of the noteworthy events involving the German-American troops and commanders were:

● Washington, D. C. was saved for the Union by the fact that after the fall of Fort Sumter (18
April 1861) 530 Pennsylvania Germans rallied around the flag and entered Washington, to shield the capital from an assault by Secessionists.

This was further enhanced by the fact that the German Turners of Baltimore firmly declared for the Union.

● Missouri was saved for the Union by German-Americans in that state. When it became known that the Secessionists planned an assault on the arsenal, the Germans of St. Louis quickly formed four companies of volunteers and took possession of the arsenal. One thousand of these Secessionists were captured on 10 May 1861, who had planned to seize the arsenal.

● The resistance at the great sacrifice by the XI Corps under Steinwehr and Schurz to the great forces of the confederates, on the first and second days of the battle of Gettysburg, enabling the Union forces to choose favorable positions.

● The brilliant work of the batteries of Dilger and Buschbek at the surprise attack by Stonewall Jackson at the battle of Chancellorsville.

● The offensive taken in the battle of Lookout Mountain and the storming of Missionary Ridge with the participation of the divisions of Osterhaus, Willich, Steinwehr, and Schurz.

● The work of Osterhaus at Pea Ridge, and his leadership of the XIV Corps in Sherman's march to the sea.

● One of the most flamboyant officers of the war was, of course, Gen. George Armstrong Custer, descended from the Germantowner, Arnold Küster, who contributed significantly to the conclusion of the Civil War.

Although primarily concentrated in the North, there were, of course, Germans settled throughout the South, and many of them served in the Confederate Army. For example, the Louisiana Germans placed eleven military companies in the field. The Virginia Germans also placed several German units into service, including the following: the Stonewall Brigade, the German Rifle Company, the Marion Rifles, and the German Home Guard. And in Charleston,

South Carolina, J. A. Wagener became the captain of the first German regiment raised there.

These are but a few examples of the German-American forces, which served in the Confederate Army. However, as noted, since most Germans were concentrated in the Northern states, their presence was most felt in the Union Army.

Symbolically, the first German-American to receive the congressional Medal of Honor did so for service in the Civil War, Private William Bensinger, who received the medal on 25 March 1863.

Whether authentic or not, no one has ever questioned the remark attributed to Robert E. Lee, "Take the Dutch out of the Union Army and we could whip the Yankees easily." Since they were one-third of the Union forces, the statement rings true.

Senator Charles Sumner said in 1862, "Our German fellow-citizens, throughout the long contest with slavery, have not only been earnest and true, but have always seen the great question in its just character and importance. Without them our cause would not have triumphed at the last Presidential election. It is only natural, therefore, that they should continue to guard and advance this cause." He also stated on the floor of the U. S. Senate, "We cannot forget the fatherland which out of its abundance has given to our republic so many good heads, so many strong arms, with so much virtue and intelligence, rejoicing in freedom and calling no man master."

Wilhelm Vocke has observed in his *Der deutsche Soldat im amerikanischen Bürgerkrieg* that the Civil War is filled with numerous examples, "In the grandest and most perilous epoch of our history, the Germans proved themselves good citizens: competent and patriotic. They brought esteem to our nation and to their ethnic heritage, a heritage exemplary for 2,000 years of loyalty and courage."

11. Service in Other Wars

In the Spanish-American War, the key naval officers were Majors Lauchheimer and Wallers, Captains Meyers and Marix and Lieutenant Schwalbe. Four rear-admirals were Winfield Schley, Louis Kempff, August Kautz, and Norman von Heldreich Farghar. The major feat of the war was accomplished by Schley, who on 3 July 1898 commanded the destruction of the Spanish fleet at Santiago, Cuba.

In World War I, the American Expeditionary Forces were commanded by General John Pershing, a descendant of German immigrants. The greatest American air hero was Eddie Rickenbacker, another German-American. One of the finest divisions was the 32nd, which was composed of German-Americans from Wisconsin and Michigan. It was one of the first divisions to engage in combat in Europe, and became known as one of America's finest. After the war it paraded down Wisconsin Ave. in Milwaukee to the applause of thousands of Milwaukee Germans.

During both world wars, one third of the troops were of German descent. This meant that in World War II one-third of the eleven million were German-Americans. It is estimated that seven hundred officers were German-American. American forces were again led by German-Americans.

Eisenhower became supreme commander of the allied forces in Europe; General Carl Spaatz was his chief adviser for the air war in Europe; Admiral Chester Nimitz was the commander-in-chief of the U. S. Pacific fleet; and General Walter Krueger was the commander of the war in the Pacific.

The first soldier to land in Europe was Private William Henke, a German-American from Minnesota, and the amphibious tanks used for D-Day were perfected by Don Roebling, a descendant of the bridge-builder, Johann August Roebling.

Of the 57,000 names listed on the Vietnam War Memorial in Washington, D. C., a full one-third are German surnames, an indication that German-American service has continued to be above that required by their percentage of the population (25%). In the American Revolution when German-Americans numbered 10% of the population, one-fourth of the American forces were German-American and since the 19th century when German-Americans have been 25% of the population, they have been over this percent of the armed forces. No statistics are as yet available for the Gulf War, however, we may note that in this war, too, American forces were again under the command of a German-American, General Norman Schwarzkopf.

Summing up German-American military service, as well as contributions to American society in general, Congressman Richard Bartholdt stated that German-Americans, "Fought for independence, opposed slavery, and loyally gave their bodies and lives that the Union might live."

III. Building the Nation

Gar vieles, was in früheren Zeiten
Ihr kaufen müsstet überm Meer,
Das lehrten wir euch selbst bereiten,
Wir stellten manche Werkstatt her.
Oh, wagt es nicht, dies zu vergessen,
Sagt nicht, als ob das nicht so sei,
Es künden's tausend Feueressen,
Da waren Deutsche auch dabei.

Und was die Kunst und Wissenschaften
Euch hier verlieh'n an Kraft und Stärk',
Es bleibt dier Ruhm am Deutschen haften,
Das meiste war der Deutschen Werk.
Und wenn aus vollen Tönen klinget
Ans Herz des Liedes Melodei,
Ich glaub' von dem, was ihr da singet,
Ist vieles Deutsche auch dabei.

***

So much of that which in earlier days
You brought here from across the sea,
We taught you how to prepare, and ways
To produce more goods, yes, 'twas we.
Dare not forget this, deny it ne'er -
Say not that we did not so do,
For a thousand forges witness bear:
At your side there were Germans too.

And though your art and your sciences now
Bring their strength and power to this land,
Their fame rests still on the German brow,
'Twas mostly done by German hand,
And when from your songs melodies ring
Memories of hearts once so true,

'Tis known to be, in the songs you sing
It is much put there by Germans too!

Konrad Krez

12. Industrial Influences

In the industrial history of the U. S., German-Americans have clearly played a major role, especially in areas which required technical training. The earlier existence in Germany of schools for training in technical fields undoubtedly was the principal cause here. The German element predominates in the engineering branches, in chemical industries, the manufacture of musical and optical instruments, the preparation of food products, as sugar and salt, cereals, flour and starch, also in canning, preserving, milling and brewing.

They have been prominent in inventing agricultural machinery, in the manufacture of wagons, electric and railway cars. From the 18th century on they have been identified with the growth of the iron and steel industries and glass manufacture; they have been prominent in printing, and have made a monopoly of the art of lithography. German-Americans have also been prominent in the clothing trade and the department stores, and their organizational skill has been evident in the area of banking and finance.

In the engineering branches especially, Germans had had in Germany first-class engineering colleges long before any were founded in the U. S. We, therefore, find that many of the greatest bridges in the country were built by Germans. Johann A. Roebling established the suspension bridge as the leading type for great spans over large rivers.

The Roeblings completed the Brooklyn Bridge in 1883; an earlier prototype had been completed across the Ohio River connecting Cincinnati, Ohio and Covington, Kentucky. Roebling's famous Brooklyn Bridge, at its completion a wonder of the world, had done greater service and has more often been overtaxed than any bridge in existence. The wire of the cables of the Roebling bridges was always manufactured in the factory of the Roebling family.

Charles C. Schneider demonstrated with his cantilever bridge over the Niagra River that the cantilever type was better for railway traffic. The beautiful George Washington Bridge over the Hudson was designed by Ammann, a Swiss-German. Joseph B. Strauss designed San Francisco's Golden Gate Bridge and was involved with 500 bridges all told.

The only peer of Edison in electrical engineering is Charles P. Steinmetz, born in Breslau. In his laboratory at Schnectady he made some brilliant discoveries and inventions, and became the consulting engineer of the General Electric Co. Called the "Wizard of Schnectady," he was responsible for more than a hundred electrical inventions.

Another German-American wizard was Edward Kleinschmidt, who invented or played a major role in the invention of the following: the teletype, the high speed stock ticker tape, the stock quotation system, the facsimile telegraph and a similar machine for radio circuits, a railroad block signal, a telephone signal system, etc. Altogether, he held 117 patents, and in 1930 sold his Teletype corporation to AT&T.

In mining engineering the name of Adolf Sutro stands out as the constructor of the great tunnel under Virginia City in Nevada. Herman Haupt, general superintendent, chief engineer and director of the Pennsylvania Railroad, built the Hoosac Tunnel. Albert Fink, expert railway engineer, was the originator of through traffic in freight and passenger service, and Count Zeppelin made his first experiments in military aviation in this country during Civil War.

William Boeing, the son of German immigrants, was the founder of the world's foremost aircraft industry, which produces commercial aircraft, such as the 727, 747, etc. The American space program was basically a creation of Wernher von Braun and his predominantly German-American scientific team, including such well known scientists as Ernst Stuhlinger.

In industrial pursuits as well as in the professions the Germans of the 19th century stood for training, preparation, or education for a particular profession. When standards were those of the pioneer, the individual might build his house with his own hands, be a successful farmer and cattle raiser, and besides be his own physician, lawyer, and legislator.

With the increase of the population and the accumulation of more than the bare necessities of existence came a higher standard of living and a higher ideal of accomplishment. Competition brought about improvement, higher effort alone was crowned with success, and this was dependent upon training.

In this emphasis upon training, the German-American has stood in opposition to the notion of the jack-of-all trades, and the adventurer in business who seeks to make money rather than to develop the industry in which he is engaged.

Swiss-Germans made great contributions to American industry, especially in grape growing (South Carolina), the production of cheese (Wisconsin), and watch-making. John Sutter, on whose vast land in California gold was discovered, was a Swiss-German, as was Louis Agassiz, one of the great names in zoology, and Felix Bloch, the Nobel prize winner in physics.

The manufacture of agricultural machinery was begun by Germans. The Buckeye mower was developed by Autelmann in Canton, Ohio. Blickensderfer, a Moravian, invented a typewriter. The first glass was produced at Jamestown in 1608. A glass factory was established near Salem, New Jersey in 1738 by Caspar Wistar from Baden. Baron Stigel set up a plant at Mannheim, Pennsylvania before the Revolution.

In the steel industry, German-Americans stand forth. The earliest known iron works, those of Gov. Spotswood at Germanna, Virginia, were operated (1714-40) by Germans from Siegen, Germany. In Pittsburgh, the first iron was made in 1792 by Georg Anschuetz from Strassburg. Other Germans developed the industry in various parts of Pennsylvania. In Bethlehem, John Fritz originated the steel mill. His product was so good that he was awarded the Bessemer gold medal by the Iron and Steel Institute of Britain.

With regard to steel, we think of Andrew Carnegie, whose two ablest lieutenants were German-Americans; Henry C. Frick and Charles M. Schwab. German specialists in chemistry, too, helped greatly in the development of the steel industry. A useful contribution by Charles T. Schoen was the invention of the pressed steel coal and freight railroad car (1897).

In other industries, such as textiles, tanning, and leather-making, the German-Americans were also active. In manufacture of vehicles John G. Brill of Kassel stands forth as the founder of one of the largest electric car and truck firms. During the 19th century, the largest vehicle factory was that of the Studebaker brothers in South Bend, Indiana.

Like the Studebakers, Walter Percy Chrysler, who founded in America's third largest auto company in 1925, comes from 18th century German immigrant stock. The Fischer Brothers were the world's biggest car body makers. One of the most highly praised antique autos today is the line of the Duesenberg Brothers' custom-built luxury cars. And the Berliner Ziebarth developed the protection system named after him.

The late Heinz Prechter served the automobile industry by becoming the premier supplier of specialty vehicles and open-air systems making the sunroof a popular option on American cars. Today, the company he founded, the American Sunroof Company is the flagship of a conglomerate of automotive, newspaper, multi-media, real estate, and investment companies with 60 facilities and 5,300 employees. He became the recipient of many awards, including distinguished German-American of the Year and the Ellis Island Medal of Honor.

Of course, an earlier German-American contribution to vehicles had been the Conestoga wagon, designed in Pennsylvania by German-Americans. It became so popular that it was used everywhere in the colonies, and became the forerunner of the prairie schooner.

Henry Villard was mainly responsible for establishing the Northern Pacific Railroad, which connected the country to the pacific northwest. In 1858, the first sleeping car for railroad travel was built by Webster Wagner from the Mohawk Valley of New York, and in 1867, he built the first drawing room car; he was also responsible for other inventions, and was elected to the state senate several times. Ship-building also engaged the inventiveness of German-American engineers - Charles H. Cramp designed the New Ironsides used in the Civil War.

As noted, German-Americans were predominant in lithography. Most of the firms engaged in this field were founded by Germans. One of them, F. A. Ringler from Hesse-Kassel, invented a galvanoplastic process which proved most serviceable in reproducing pictures. The great contribution, however, to newspaper production was the linotype machine, invented by Ottmar Mergenthaler from Württemberg. The *New York Tribune* was the first daily to introduce this machine in its type-setting room.

German-Americans also played a major role in the manufacture of musical instruments. Some of the finest violins were produced by Georg Gemuender of Würtemberg. At the London Exposition of 1851, they took first prize. In the area of pianos, German-Americans have been predominant: Playel, Erhardt, Behrent, Steinway, Weber, Steck, Kranich & Bach, Sohmer, Behr, Schnabel, and Knabe. The first piano made in the colonies was in 1775 in Philadelphia by Georg Behrent. Henry Steinway and his four sons arrived in New York in mid-19th century, and began manufacturing pianos, which set the standard for superb quality. Franz Rudolph Wurlitzer of Saxony founded the dynasty of theater organ and jukebox builders.

Other German-American products include the pencils of Eberhard Faber and the Welsbach lamp, the latter of which revolutionized the street-lighting of larger cities. From Wilhelm Rittenhouse, builder of the first American paper mill (1690) in Germantown, Pennsylvania, to Frederick Wyerhaeuser's family, German-Americans were instrumental in the development of the country's forest and paper product industries.

In the east, the names of two large department stores were those of Wanamaker and Siegel-Cooper. John Wanamaker, a Pennsylvania German, established his first store in Philadelphia in 1876. In 1899, Sebastian Kresge opened his first general store in Detroit, and went on to become the "Dime Store King," and his stores today form the chain known as "K-Mart."

German-Americans also became well known in the food processing and packing industries. The name of Heinz of the "57" varieties belongs to a company founded by Henry J. Heinz. The manufacture of oatmeal, or rolled oats, for breakfast was originated in 1856 by Ferdinand Schumacher of Hannover. Claus Spreckels, also of Hannover, became a success in California as the so-called "sugar king" of the Pacific Coast.

Later, he organized the beet-sugar industry, which competed with the sugar refineries of the east. Spreckels also was involved in banking, railroad building, and the construction of gas and electric plants. Another prominent family in the sugar industry was that of the Havemeyers. William Havemeyer came from Germany in 1799. Brand names connected with the food industry are those of Mueller, Redenbacher, Gerber, Oscar Meyer, Hellmann, Entenmann, and of course, Kraft, Kroger, and the Hershey family of Pennsylvania.

Mention might also be made of the influence on American foods, much of which is of German origin. For example, two items which carry the names of the German cities they came from, are some of the most popular food items in the U.S.: frankfurters and hamburgers. Also, bratwurst has gained tremendous popularity in recent years. In the area of brewing, of course, German-Americans have always predominated with such names as: Anheuser-Busch, Stroh, Schell, Hudepohl, Schlitz, Miller, Coors, Shaefer, Heilmann, Pabst, Blatz...

Finally, a comment should be made on the German-American work ethic. Historically, German-Americans viewed work at the basis for the support of the family unit, rather than merely as the means of obtaining wealth for the individual. They, therefore, stressed careful investment and high rates of savings, rather than speculative business practices. In workmanship they believed in the careful accomplishment of a defined task, and believed in the value of work for its own sake, rather than the monetary value placed on it.

In the pharmaceutical industry, Max Kade made lasting contributions, and became one of those German-Americans who embodied the American Dream. As the manufacturer of a cough medicine "Pertussin," which is well known to this day by parents and children across the country, he became a giant in his field of endeavor. Moreover, he was especially interested in German-American relations. In 1944, he and his wife, Annette, established the Max Kade Foundation, which helped build student dormitories, libraries, and other meeting places for those in the academic community. Among his major contributions were the support of centers, institutes and libraries devoted to the field of German-American Studies, such as, for example, the German-Americana Collection at the University of Cincinnati, and the institutes at the at the University of Kansas, the Indiana University-Purdue University at Indianapolis, and the Pennsylvania State University.

13. Social Influences

Another contribution to American life has been in the area of social life. European travelers in the 18th and early 19th century were appalled by the gravity, melancholy, and monotony of American social life. For example, Mrs. Trollope, returning from her residence in America (1827-31), wrote that she had never seen a population so totally divested of gaiety, and she quotes a German woman as saying: "they do not love music; and they never amuse themselves; and their hearts are not warm, at least they seem so to strangers; and they have no ease, no forgetfulness of business and of care, no not for a moment."

The importance of social life is underscored in a 19th century German-American guidebook, *Der Goldne Wegweiser* (The Golden Signpost), which expressed a great deal of the German-American viewpoint on a wide variety of topics. With regard to social life, it indicated that "hospitality and cheerful social relations should actually be just an extension of family life, and if friendship is only possible between a few, we can still associate with many."

It noted that social life "becomes a real refreshment of everyday existence" and that "truly noble and cheering pleasures change the fleeting hours to unforgettable ones, they make them an enduring monument, so to speak, and are a means of education that should not be underestimated."

Germans, hence, brought with them a large capacity for the enjoyment of life; they had their agricultural fairs and frolics in the 18th century and expanded them to festivals on a large scale as time went on. A word commonly used to describe German-American social life is "Gemütlichkeit," which is defined as the quality of a "good natured, sanguine, easy-going disposition." To German-Americans, the word signifies all that and more, as it refers to a basic outlook on life and way of living. It means that they go out of their way to maximize their enjoyment of life in the area of social activities, an attribute which is best characterized by the plethora of German-American festivities.

Today, German-American festivities range from summer fests to Oktoberfest. Aside from the numerous German-American festivities, German-Americans also Germanized American ones. The Fourth of July, for example, very well reflects the German impact, as German-Americans turned it into a festive occasion, with not only fireworks, but cannons and rifle-shooting societies participating as well. In Cincinnati, the children went trick-and-treating on Halloween, but when they came to the door, they asked for "Küchele," which is German for donut

German-Americans also founded numerous social and cultural organizations most varied in kind - ranging from singing societies to literary clubs for entertainment and enlightenment. They introduced numerous customs and traditions - ranging from the Easter Bunny to the Christmas Tree. Indeed they made Christmas the principal festivity of the year, and they gave delight to the young with a flood of toys, designed with consummate skill and fascinating workmanship, from the indestructible picture-book to the doll with movable joints, from the tin soldiers to the self-propelling man-of-war, from Noah's Ark to the Teddy Bear (an invention of Margarete Steiff, of Württemberg).

It should also be noted that in German-American families there is a great deal of preparation and merrymaking when it comes to the celebration of birthdays, betrothals, and weddings. Annual family reunions have also proved to be popular recently.

Finally, it should be noted with regard to family life that German-Americans historically celebrated the patriarchal family, and one in which women and children all worked together for the common good of the family. Families not only worked together, they enjoyed their social life together. They also recognized life-long obligations between parent and child. Historically, German-American families were characterized by the following: first, they were larger than the average family. Second, German-Americans more often married and resided in areas near their extended family, and enjoyed high rates of home ownership. Third, children began to work at an earlier age and contributed their earnings to the welfare of the family. And, fourth, women assisted the family enterprise either at home or by working, but the view was with regard to assisting the family as a basic cooperative economic venture, and one in which each member of the family has a contribution to make.

14. Educational Influences

German thought and practice have exerted a great deal of influence on American education. These influences were transmitted not only by German-Americans, but by persons of other ethnic backgrounds, who had either studied in Germany, had traveled there, or maintained correspondence with German educators and intellectuals. The entire educational system from kindergarten to university was deeply influenced and patterned after German educational models.

These influences began early on in American history. Cotton Mather, the famous New England divine, corresponded in Latin with August Hermann Francke, the noted philanthropist who established the first model orphanage in Halle, Germany. This was an example of the Anglo-German intellectual exchange, which would take place between leading thinkers in both countries, and contributed to the flow of ideas to the New World from Germany.

In Pennsylvania, the Germans maintained their own schools in which German was the language of instruction. Their most distinguished teacher was Franz Daniel Pastorius, the founder of Germantown. He served as burgomaster and leading educator. The school he established in 1702 even had an evening program for those who worked during the day. Another German-American who distinguished himself in the classroom was Christopher Dock, a Mennonite. He introduced the blackboard into the American classroom, which became a basic element of instruction. In 1750, he also published the first pedagogic work in America. In 1764, he published his well-known "One Hundred Necessary Rules of Conduct for Children," which provided some basic rules and guidelines for how children should behave themselves.

A number of educators in the colonies went to Germany, and became acquainted with the educational system there. One of the earliest to visit a German university was Benjamin Franklin. In 1776, he attended a meeting of the Royal Society of Science in Göttingen, and became a member thereof. Another American from Philadelphia who visited Göttinggen was Benjamin Smith Barton, who obtained his M.D. in 1789 at the university. Upon his return to Philadelphia he became a well-known physician. He was among the first of many Americans who would obtain their education at a German university.

In the 19th century, many more began to attend German universities, and upon their return they exerted a strong influence in terms of introducing German educational ideas, methods, and practices. Ticknor, and Longfellow who followed him, used the German university model in organizing their language department at Harvard. Among the teachers that Longfellow hired, the most outstanding was Carl Follen, a cultured political refugee and later a Unitarian minister, who became the first professor of German in the U.S. at Harvard (1831-36).

Interest in German educational methods was greatly enhanced by a French brochure, which was a report on the Prussian schools, published in 1832 by the well-known philosopher Victor Cousin. Through this extremely favorable report the school board of Ohio was induced to send the Rev. Calvin E. Stowe, the husband of Harriet Beecher Stowe, abroad to make a closer study of German education. His enthusiastic report published in 1836, gave a detailed account of what he had observed.

Another American educator who gave high praise to German schools was Horace Mann of Massachusetts. His unbounded admiration of the preparation of teachers inspired him to organize the first American normal school in 1839. In his book on Mann,

Burke Hinsdale noted that, "It is Germany that in this century has exerted upon our country the most protracted, the deepest and the most salutary educational influence." Mann's famous *Seventh Annual Report* (1843) highly praised the Prussian schools. Mann was especially impressed with the training of the teachers, their kindness, and the absence of corporal punishment.

One of the profoundest educational influences came through the works and writings of Johann Friedrich Herbart, a professor at Göttingen. It was he who introduced psychology into teaching.

Enthusiastic American educators founded the first Herbartian Club in 1892. The German educator's ideas and methods were widely adopted throughout the nation. Bancroft, who had been impressed with German methods of teaching, aimed to introduce them in New England. Together with Cogswell, he founded the Round Hill School in 1823 near Northampton, Massachusetts. Another American educator who observed schools abroad was John Griscom, who visited Pestalozzi in Switzerland. Thomas Jefferson said that Griscom's report gave him valuable ideas in organizing the University of Virginia.

Efforts to use the German university as a model were particularly pronounced in Michigan. Several of the early university presidents there were tireless in their endeavors to follow the German model. A university in the East which reflected the German model was Cornell, founded in 1868. Its first president, Andrew D. White, had served as U.S. Minister to Germany from 1879-81. He was impressed with what he saw in Germany. He was guided by the German university model as he helped establish Cornell University.

White was especially interested in building up technical education, and it is no doubt due to this influence that the first school of forestry in the U.S. was established at Cornell. German influences were also strong at Johns Hopkins University, which was founded in 1876. Almost all of the members of its faculty had obtained their doctoral degrees in Germany. Stanford University's first president Professor Jordan, who had studied in Germany, chose as a motto for his institution: "Die Luft der Freiheit weht," or "Freedom is in the Air," a reference to academic freedom.

American education was, however, not only influenced at the upper levels, but at the lower ones as well. The kindergarten - the very term itself is German - which had been founded in Germany by Friedrich Froebel, was introduced into this country by the wife of Carl Schurz at Watertown, Wisconsin in 1855.

In most areas where German-Americans were settled, German instruction could be found. Although private and parochial schools offered German instruction in the colonial era, it was not until 1840 in Cincinnati that the first German bilingual public school programs were established, thus earning for it the title as the home of German bilingual instruction in the U.S.

Thereafter, similar public school programs spread throughout the country. These programs were established upon the request of the public based on the model in Ohio, where the legislature had directed all boards of education to introduce German instruction whenever it was requested by at least 75 citizens. German-Americans, hence, created and established bilingual education in America, something which today is quite common across the country - this is a German-American contribution.

German was taught in elementary schools across the country well into the 20th century. Until 1918, there was a German Department in the Cincinnati Public Schools, which was under the direction of Dr. H. H. Fick, who published a series of textbooks which were used in German bilingual programs across the U.S. Before the First World War Fick's program consisted of 250 teachers of German with more than 15,000 students of German. A typical book used in the program was Fick's *Neu und Alt: Ein Buch für die Jugend* (1911).

During the latter quarter of the 19th century a new educational influence came from Germany, which had a marked effect on the American school system. This was vocational education. Germany had had great success with its trade schools and they were eagerly imitated by other European nations. Americans, too, became interested and German practices were soon introduced here. Pioneering the combination of academic and vocational education was the Charles E. Emmerich Manual Training High School of Indianapolis in 1894. Today, vocational education is commonplace in the educational curriculum - it is a German-American contribution.

One feature of German education which has greatly influenced American schools is physical education. In 1811, Friedrich Ludwig Jahn had started what was known as "Turnerei," a movement to make young Germans vigorous in body and mind. In fact the motto was "a sound body and a sound mind."

Through Carl Beck and Carl Follen it spread to New England, being introduced at the Round Hill School in Northampton, Massachusetts. And Francis Lieber set up the first swimming pool in Boston. Like bilingual and vocational education, physical education is another German-American contribution to the curriculum.

The Turner movement spread swiftly in the U.S., especially after the arrival of several thousand refugees of the failed 1848 Revolution in Germany. In Cincinnati, the first Turnverein was established in 1848, and thereafter, many more were established across the country. Almost every German-American community had its own Turnverein. Public education was influenced by the movement, as German-Americans strongly recommended that physical education become a part of the curriculum of the schools. Milwaukee and later Indianapolis housed the German Normal School for the training of physical education teachers.

Every school building had to have a gymnasium, and physical training became a basic element of the program of the YMCA. Gymnastics and physical training were a major German contribution to American education.

Finally, reference should be made to the various centers, collections, and institutes at colleges and universities, which deal with the field of German-American Studies, including, for example, the Max Kade Institutes at the University of Wisconsin-Madison, the University of Kansas, Indiana University-Purdue University at Indianapolis, and Pennsylvania State University; the University of Cincinnati's German-Americana collection; and the Germans from Russian Heritage Collection at North Dakota State University.

15. Musical Influences

German-speaking immigrants co-created America's musical landscape from the village band and the singing societies to the great symphony orchestras.

It has been said that had German-Americans done nothing more than to have brought music to America, that this would have been a major contribution to American life. *Der Goldne Wegweiser* (The Golden Signpost), commented on the significance of music, stating that "what words are not able to utter, musical sound reechoes; it gives expression to the highest and the profoundest feelings of the human breast; it mirrors the tenderest emotions, the most secret moods of the heart - it expresses the soul of the soul."

During the 18th century, the Puritans in New England and the Quakers in Pennsylvania checked the development of music. Contemporaneously, the German sectarians of Pennsylvania, though austere in their mode of life, fondly practiced the art of choral singing.

The mixed chorus of the brothers and sisters of Ephrata, and the music schools of the Moravians at Bethlehem invoked admiration, and fostered the sacred flame. Philadelphia with its large German population early on began the cultivation of music and gave the first ambitious program of classical music on 4 May 1786. A noteworthy accomplishment was made in Boston with the founding of the Handel and Haydn Society in 1815. Its principal conductor from 1854 to 1895, Carl Zerrahn, left a lasting legacy in the development of choral and orchestral music in America. He was succeeded by another German-American, Emil Mollehnauer.

Johann Graupner earlier had won the distinction of having established the Philharmonic Society in Boston in 1810/11, which became one of the finest orchestras of its time. For this reason

Graupner is considered the father of orchestral music in America. New York began to show its mettle about the middle of the century with the foundation of the Philharmonic Society. Its rival, the famous Germania Orchestra, boldly began to make tours, giving orchestral concerts in many of the eastern cities between 1848 and 1854.

There then came the period of the great German masters: Theodor Thomas, Anton Seidl, Leopold Damrosch, Wilhelm Gericke, Emil Paur, and many others, who developed a musical taste for the symphony, and the grand opera.

Their tradition was continued by Bruno Walter, Otto Klemperer, Fritz Reiner, Fritz Kreisler, Max Rudolf, and William Steinberg. Current German conductors include Erich Kunzel of the Cincinnati Symphony Orchestra and Kurt Masur of the New York Philharmonic Orchestra.

From Yankee Doodle to Parsifal has been the record of German influence upon musical appreciation in the U.S. In vocal music the efforts of the German-American singing societies must not be overlooked. They continue to sponsor Sängerfeste, and have contributed greatly to the preservation of the German heritage by means of their use of the German language. Especially influential were the conservatories and private music schools, very frequently founded or directed by German professors of music. Among the many opera singers whose names stand forth are: Ernestine Schumann-Heink, Lotte Lehmann, and Elisabeth Schwarzkopf.

John Phillip Sousa (1854-1932), whose mother was from Germany, became a conductor of the Marine Band at age twenty-four. As a composer of marches, he is unequaled in the world. Few melodies touch Americans more than his "Stars and Stripes Forever."

Finally, reference should be made to Georg Drumm, who composed "Hail America" during the height of the Anti-German Hysteria of World War I in order to calm the frenzy. This ceremonial march was re-named "Hail to the Chief" in 1952, when it was first used for official purposes in the Eisenhower administration. Since that time, Drumm's march has become the leitmotif that "drums up" an impending entry on stage for all U.S. presidents.

Bach, Haendel, Haydn, Mozart, Beethoven, Schubert, Schumann, Brahms, Weber, Wagner, Mahler, and Strauss are but a few of the names of the German musical heritage, which has so greatly enriched the musical life of America. A great deal of what is called "classical" music is actually of German origin. German-American conductors, musicians infused the cultural life of America with this musical dimension.

16. Artistic Influences

Strong German-American influences can be found in all branches of art. We can allude to only a few outstanding artists here. In painting, German influences have been quite strong. Among the early painters the most distinguished was Emanuel Leutze from Würtemberg, whose best known work is "Washington Crossing the Delaware," (1851). Interestingly, this famous historic painting was completed in Düsseldorf on the Rhine and the Continentals in the boat were painted from German models. Hence, it would be possible to call the painting "Washington Crossing the Rhine."

Another well known work by Leutze is "Westward the Course of Empire Takes Its Way," which is located in the U.S. House of Representatives. A magnificent fresco, 20' x 30,' depicts the pioneers moving west on the frontier. This work in the nation's capital is one of the many German-American works of art in Washington, D. C. Many references to them can be found in *Art in the United States Capital: Prepared by the Architect of the Capitol under the Direction of the Joint Committee on the Library.* (1976)

Prior to Paris and Munich, Düsseldorf had a predominating influence on these early American painters. Albert Bierstadt, who studied there, upon his return to America became fascinated by the Wild West. He produced numerous paintings of exceptional grace and beauty. These included works depicting the Rocky Mountains, the Yosemite and the Sierras.

The importance of German-American artists in the shaping of the American image of the American West is underscored by the fact that of the 25 American artists whose works are displayed at the Buffalo Bill Historical Center in Cody, Wyoming, 11 are German-American, or 44% of the artists! These include: Karl Bodmer, Alfred Jacob Miller, Albert Bierstadt, Charles Schreyvogel, Olaf Seltzer,

Edward Borein, William Henry Koerner, Winold Reiss, Carl Rungius, and Nick Eggenhoffer. We may well conclude that the image we have of the American West was strongly influenced by German-American artists.

Information on them can be found in Peter C.Merrill, *German Immigrant Artists in America: A Biographical Dictionary* (1997). Reference should also be made to the American-born German-American artists, who have played an important role in the history of American art. For example, the Minnesota Historical Society dubbed Adolf Dehn "Minnesota's artist." He is noted as the "father of lithography, almost solely responsible for the development of the art-print process, and his versatile talents included watercolors, silk screen, fabric, and oils. A collection of his works can be found in *Adolf Dehn Drawings* (1971), which contains his sketches and drawings of Minnesota, New York, and Vienna.

Several of the numerous German-American sculptors dealt with German-American historical topics. Karl Bitter completed a large number of statues, monuments, and portrait-busts, the most outstanding of which were those of General Franz Sigel and Carl Schurz, both located in New York. By J. Otto Schweizer is a statue of General Peter Mühlenberg for the front of the City Hall in Philadelphia; the Steuben monuments at Utica, New York and Valley Forge; the Schiller Monument in Buffalo, New York; and the Molly Pitcher Monument in Carlisle, New Jersey. In Minnesota, the exquisite wood sculpture of the Swiss-German, Ulrich Steiner, adorns numerous locales.

An artist whose works came to define the German-American experience in a sculptural sense was Albert Jaegers. His Founders Monument in commemoration of the landing of the German settlers of Germantown is located in Germantown, Pennsylvania. It depicts the arrival of the founders of the first all-German settlement in

America. On the sides and rear of the pedestal reliefs reveal the important role German-Americans have had in the making of America. In the one relief, physical labor is shown as the fundamental principle upon which art and science arise. Another shows the war volunteer, who freely sheds his blood for the independence and Union of his country. The last one shows the protests made against slavery by Germantowners in 1688. Often forgotten, and located in what is now a slum, the Founders Monument captures the essence of German-Americans actively involved in all aspects of settling, building, and preserving the Union.

The most well-known statue in the U.S. - the Statue of Liberty was created by a sculptor of ethnic German stock. Dedicated in 1886, the statue was titled in full "Liberty Enlightening the World." It was the creation of Frederic-Auguste Bartholdi, born in Kolmar in the province of Alsace.

In architecture, German-Americans have distinguished themselves also. Thomas U. Walter was appointed in 1851 by President Fillmore to superintend the extension of the Capitol in Washington. He designed the great iron dome and a number of public buildings, including the U.S. Treasury and the wings of the Patent Office. The Library of Congress was designed by architects Smithmeyer and Pelz in 1886. G. L. Heinz was the architect for the cathedral of St. John the Divine in New York. Since the 1930s, members of the Bauhaus school of architecture became influential in the U. S., notably Walter Gropius and Mies van der Rohe, who had left the Third Reich in protest. Recently, Helmut Jahn of Chicago has become internationally well known for his architectural work.

German-Americans contributed to the art of illustrating and engraving, and the name of Alfred Stieglitz is known for his development of artistic expression by means of photography. Comic illustration and cartooning were brought to a high level by Thomas Nast, born in Landau. His brilliant cartoons in defense of the Civil War evoked praise from President Lincoln. His caricatures were not merely entertaining; they also had a serious message. In New York, he fought against corruption of Tammany Hall with his vitriolic caricatures. As a creator of American symbols, he has no equal.

Among his numerous cartoon creations were the donkey for the Democratic Party, the elephant for the Republican Party, the image of Uncle Sam, as well as the popular image of Santa Claus. Another cartoonist, almost as influential as Nast, was Joseph Keppler from Vienna, the founder of *Puck*. Equally effective was the caricaturist of *Judge*, Eugene Zimmermann. Following the *Katzenjammer Kids* by Rudi Dicks, the comic series *Peanuts*, by Charles Schultz became a popular feature of the press.

It is evident that a history of American art would be incomplete without reference to the substantial number of German-American painters, sculptors, and architects, whose works number among the great treasures of the New World.

17. Film Influences

An introduction to the role played by German-Americans in the film industry can be found in Cornelius Schnauber's *German-Speaking Artists in Hollywood: Emigration Between 1910 and 1945* (1996). German-speaking immigrants and their offspring were involved early on in the film industry, going back to the very beginnings in the era of the silent screen.

In 1912, Carl Laemmle acquired the Nestor Company, which had the first film studio in Hollywood, and made this the basis of his well-known Universal Studios. One of the first actors he contracted was Vienna-born Erich von Stroheim, who became a great actor, as well as film director. According to Schnauber, he "introduced formal and contextual elements into movie-making which were demonstrably influenced by the literature of German Naturalism, Austrian Fin de Siecle, and German Expressionism."

Ernst Lubitsch became one of the major film directors, whose films were noted for their sophistication and witty comedy. Other notable film directors include Josef von Sternberg, Billy Wilder, Fritz Lang, Edgar Ulmer, John Brahm, Douglas Sirk, and Fred Zinnemann. It is beyond the scope of this work to even to begin to list their many films, but some of the classics include: Billy Wilder's *Sunset Boulevard* (1950), Fritz Lang's *The Big Heat* (1952), and Fred Zinnemann's *High Noon* (1952).

Among the many well-known actors mention may be made of: Marlene Dietrich, Peter Lorre, Paul Henried, Conrad Veidt, and Walter Slezak. Perhaps best known of the American-born actors of German descent are Clark Gable and Doris Kapellhoff Day. More recently, this list would have to be added to with names, such as: Oscar Werner, Horst Buchholz, Elke Sommer, Curt Juergens, Wim

Wenders, Werner Klemperer, Arnold Schwarzenegger, Maximillian Schell, and Eric Braeden.

German-Americans have been involved, however, not only as actors and directors, but in all aspects of the film industry. Max Steiner, for example, was responsible for the memorable score for *Gone with the Wind* (1938). Further information on German-Americans in the film industry can be found in Charles R. Haller's *Distinguished German-Americans* (1995).

18. Political Influences

From Peter Minuit, Jacob Leisler and Franz Daniel Pastorius in the 17th century to Henry Kissinger in the 20th, German-Americans have taken an active role in American political life. However, the first politician who emerged as a real national spokesman of German-Americans was Carl Schurz, who began his long career in the 1850s.

The life of Schurz is recorded in his fascinating three-volume memoirs, and his life's work is well presented in the six-volume edition of his speeches and memoirs, edited by Frederic Bancroft. The first great service of Schurz in American politics was his brilliant public speaking in opposition to the institution of slavery. He opened a new line of attack against slavery, not in the manner of native orators, who rang the charges of an outraged humanity, or appealed to that sacrosanct document, the American Constitution, but he pointed to the economic decline of the Southern states in comparison with the sound economic condition of the North based on free labor.

He appealed more to intelligence than to the emotions of prejudices. He spoke equally well in English and in German, drew great audiences in Boston and New York, as easily as in Wisconsin or Minnesota, he was one of the most effective orators in the Lincoln campaign and a great factor in the victory of the Republican Party in 1860. Appointed Ambassador to Spain in recognition of his services, Schurz resigned at the outbreak of the war, in order to enter the Union Army. He distinguished himself as a commander at the battle of Gettysburg and at Lookout Mountain.

His oratorical powers were enlisted in the campaign for the re-election of Lincoln. Immediately after the war he was sent to observe the condition of the South, and his report is a classic of contemporary history. Elected to the honor of membership in the U. S. Senate by the State of Missouri, Schurz was noted as one of the Senate's most brilliant orators, an uncompromising idealist, and a caustic critic. His next great achievement was his work for civil service reform. He was chosen by President Hayes as a member of his cabinet, receiving the post of Secretary of the Interior. In this position, he for the first time in American history, carried out the principles of civil service reform.

The standard of efficiency was the only one which kept a person under Schurz in office. Republicans and Democrats were treated alike. In carrying out this great principle Schurz incurred so much opposition and hostility in his own party that he destroyed himself politically. No public officer had ever dared to take this uncompromising a stand. President Grant had shrunk from it, the next President brave enough to try the experiment of civil service reform was Grover Cleveland. Schurz had driven a wedge, but he suffered martyrdom for it. When he left the cabinet, he was politically dead, and was, henceforth, an independent in politics.

Though one of the pillars of the Republican Party in its earliest days, he turned against Grant for the second term, and subsequently supported Grover Cleveland with enthusiasm, withdrawing his support, however, at a later day, when the Democratic party identified itself with the free silver agitation.

Schurz, hence, established an outstanding political record, which was based on principles rather than party politics. Schurz clearly represents the German-American active on the national stage of American politics. Secretary of State Henry Kissinger followed in Schurz's footsteps in the 20th century as a German-born member of the Presidential Cabinet.

In the 20th century, two presidents were of German descent: Herbert Hoover and Dwight D. Eisenhower. Also, there have been numerous congressional representatives from German-American stock, including Senator Robert Wagner of New York, Senator Everett Dirksen of Illinois, and Representative Thomas Luken of Cincinnati.

With regard to German-American political viewpoints in general, it should be noted that historically German-Americans have stressed the important qualities of the candidate and his/her principles, rather than the political party the candidate belongs to. They often claimed that the Yankees supported the party, rather than examining the individual running for office. They expected good and clean government, which reflected both the religious and the political, especially the 48er, heritage of the German-Americans.

German-Americans historically have had strong beliefs about the role of government, whose central role they felt was to guarantee and to protect "persönliche Freiheit" (personal liberty). Government should, therefore, guarantee the individual's personal liberty to the fullest measure in accordance with the principles of basic law and order. This meant that any attempts to legislate the individual's personal liberty by laws, such as prohibition, would be regarded as an invasion of individual liberty. Such views continue to hold true today with regard to the German-American viewpoint in the political realm.

Among the political issues in American history in which German-Americans have been particularly influential were the following: 1. the abolition of slavery; 2. the reform of the civil service system; 3. the maintenance of a sound-money standard; 4. the reform of political parties; 5. questions of personal liberty; 6. independent voting; 7. the rights of workers; 8. bilingual education; 9. progressive legislation, including social security; and 10. environmental responsibility.

The platform of the national German-American Alliance, which was adopted before the First World War, may be seen as representative of where German-Americans stood historically with regard to a number of issues. The platform of the Alliance contained the following points:

1. The Alliance, as such, refrains from all interference in party politics, reserving, however, the right and duty to defend its principles also in the political field, in case these should be attacked or endangered by political measures. The Alliance will inaugurate and support all legislation for the common good that is sure to find unanimous approval of its members.

2. Questlons and matters of religion are strictly excluded.

3. It recommends the introduction of the study of German into the public schools on the following broad basis: along with English, German is a world language; wherever the pioneers of civilization, trade and commerce have penetrated, we find people of both languages represented; wherever real knowledge of another language prevails more generally, there an independent, clear and unprejudiced understanding is more easily formed and mutual friendly relations promoted.

4. We live in an age of progress and invention; the pace of our time is rapid, and the demands on the individual are inexorable; the physical exertion involved increases the demand on the bodily force; a healthy mind should live in a healthy body. For these reasons the Alliance will labor for the introduction of systematic and practical gymnastic (physical culture) instruction in the public schools.

5. It further declares in favor of taking the school out of politics, for only a system of education that is free from political influence can offer the people real and satisfactory schools.

6. It calls on all Germans to acquire the right of citizenship as soon as they are legally entitled to it, to take an active part in public

life, and to exercise their right at the polls fearlessly and according to their own judgement.

7. It recommends either a liberal and modern interpretation or the abolition of laws, that put unnecessary difficulties in the way of acquiring the right of citizenship, and the frequently entirely prevent it. Good character, unblamable upright life, obedience to laws should decide, and not the answering or non-answering of arbitrarily selected political or historical questions, which easily confuse the applicant.

8. It opposes any and every restriction of immigration of healthy persons from Europe, exclusive of convicted criminals and anarchists.

9. It favors the abolition of antiquated laws no longer in accordance with the spirit of the times, which check free intercourse and restrict the personal freedom of the citizen, and recommends a sane regulation of the liquor traffic in conformity with good common sense and high ethical principles.

10. It recommends the founding of educational societies, which will foster the German language and literature, teach those anxious to learn and arrange courses and lectures on art and science and questions of general interest.

11. It recommends a systematic investigation of the share Germans have had in the development of the U.S., in war and peace, in all kinds of German-American activity, from the earliest days, as the basis for the founding and continuance of German-American history.

12. The alliance advocates all legal and economically correct measures for the protection of the forests of the U. S.

13. We deem it our duty to assist as much as possible original ideas and inventions of German-Americans for the common good of our country.

14. It reserves the right to extend or supplement this platform when new conditions within the scope of its time and aims make it desirable or necessary.

Taken together these points may be viewed as reflecting much of the historical roots of where German-Americans stood on a variety of issues. With regard to their contribution to the political life of America in general, Congressman Richard Bartholdt commented that German-Americans historically have been, "imbued with the American spirit of freedom to such an extent that they love liberty better than whatever good might come from its restriction. As a rule, they modestly refrained from seeking political preferment but filled America's life with music, song and innocent social pleasures. They are peaceful and law-abiding citizens, who by industry and thrift have made the best of the opportunities . . . and thus they have contributed their honest share to the growth, the development, and the grandeur of the Republic."

20. Literary Influences

German-American Literature refers to the vast body of writings in the German and English languages by German-American authors. Since the 17th century there have been over 3,000 of them, and their works have been recorded in Robert E. Ward's *A Bio-Bibliography of German-American Creative Writers, 1670-1970* (1985).

Among the significant colonial authors were: Franz Daniel Pastorius and Johann Conrad Beissel. In the 19th century there were numerous writers, some of whose works became well known on both sides of the Atlantic. Karl Postl (pseudonym: Charles Sealsfield) even became a best-selling author of the mid-19th century in both America and Germany.

Other well-known 19th century authors were: Caspar Butz, Martin Drescher, Karl Knortz, Konrad Krez, Konrad Nies, Heinrich A. Rattermann, Robert Reitzel, Ernst Anton Zuendt. Leading authors in the early 20th century were: H. H. Fick, Georg Sylvester Viereck, Theodore Dreiser and Otto Oscar Kollbrunner.

In the 1930s, many German authors came as emigres to America, and some remained and became U. S. citizens. Among the better known of this group of German-American authors was, of course, Nobel Prize winner Thomas Mann, who wrote some of his major works after he had become a U. S. citizen.

In the 1970s the Assoication of German-Language Authors in America published a poetry series, as well as a literary journal, *Zeitschrift für deutschamerikanische Literatur*.

Currently, there is a series, *Deutschschreibende Autoren in Nordamerika*, which has published the work of German-language authors, such as Irmgard Elsner Hunt, Gert Niers, Peter Pabisch, and others.

There is also a literary organization, the Society for Contemporary Literature in German, which publishes a journal, *Trans-Lit*. Here one finds the works of contemporary German-American authors, such as Peter Beicken, Lisa Kahn, Ingeborg Carsten-Miller, and Margot Scharpenberg.

Three of the most well-known German-American authors were L. Frank Baum, who wrote The Wizard of Oz; Theodore S. Geisel, author of children's literature who wrote more than fifty books, including the famous Dr. Seuss books, such as *The Cat in the Hat*. (his works sold more than 100 million copies and have been translated into twenty languages, including Braille); and Max Ehrmann, who is well known for his prose poem "Desiderata."

For obvious reasons, the vast majority of German-American authors of the 20th century have been writing in the language of the country in English.

These include Carol Ascher, Thomas Berger, Pearl S. Buck, Charles Bukowski, Theodore Dreiser, Stuart Friebert, John Gunther, Joseph Hergesheimer, Norbert Krapf, Ludwig Lewisohn, H. L. Mencken, Joaquin Miller, Lisel Mueller, Charles Nordhoff, Conrad Richter, John Godfrey Saxe, Herman George Scheffauer, Gertrude Stein, Ruth Suckow, Bayard Taylor, Henry Timrod, Leon Uris, Kurt Vonnegut, and Paula Weber. Many of these are authors of major importance, whose works illuminate various aspects of the German-American experience.

One might notice the influence of German literature when reading the works of American authors, such as Cooper, Irving, Poe, Longfellow, Whittier, Thoreau, Melville, Whitman, or Twain, it is because many of them actually were influenced by German culture by means of travels in the German-speaking countries or by the reading of German literature. The early history of this fascinating chapter of cross-cultural relations between Germany and America is traced in an encyclopedic work by Henry A. Pochmann, *German Culture in America: Philosophical and Literary Influences, 1600-1900* (1957).

In relation to literary influences and the significance of books, *Der Goldne Wegweiser* (*The Golden Signpost*) advised that "everyone should have books. A house without books is rightly called a literary desert." It also advised that "If you have accumulated a number of books, it is most important that you use them well and preserve them well. By good use we mean not reading them through superficially, but rather studying them carefully. A book that is not worth reading twice is not worth reading at all. Take good care of your books."

21. Linguistic Influences

English is a Germanic language of the Indo-European language family. The Germanic languages are divided into three sub-groups: East (all of these are extinct); North (the Scandinavian languages); and West. English itself contains numerous words of German origin. American English, or as H. L. Mencken called it, American, has also incorporated the influences of many languages, especially those brought to America by various immigrant groups. Mencken wrote that the German have left an indelible mark on America, especially on English as it is spoken in the U.S. Indeed, everyday vocabulary displays many German words and phrases. Hence, we find that American English not only has many words of German origin, but that it also contains numerous loanwords, which have been taken directly into the American vocabulary, and reflect the linguistic impact of the German immigrations.

German loanwords can be found in all possible areas. It shows in the area pertaining to dietary ingredients. This in itself is an indication of how German food ways have deeply influenced the American diet. Indeed, the influence has been so great that German words were incorporated directly into the everyday language. These words are so ingrained in the vocabulary, because they refer to some basic elements of the diet in America. Hence, making both a linguistic and dietary impact.

A few of these German loanwords, from a variety of areas are as follows: angst, auslese, bedeckt, beergarden, bierstube, bismarck, blitzkreig, bock beer, bratwurst, cole slaw (Kohlsalat), concertmaster, cookbook, dachshund, delicatessen, dummkopf, edelweiss, ersatz, flak, fahrvergnuegen, frankfurter, gemuetlichkeit, gestalt, gesundheit, glockenspiel, gummi bear, hamburger, hasenpfeffer, hausfrau, hinterland, iceberg, kaffeeklatsch, kaputt, katzenjammer, kitsch, Kriss Kringle, kuchen, lager beer, leitmotif, liebfraumilch, lied, marzipan, meerschaum, misch-masch, mettwurst, muesli, noodle, ohm, ostpolitik, paraffin, pfannkuchen, plunder, poltergeist, pretzel, prosit, pumpernickel, rathskeller, riesling, rucksack, sauerbraten, sauerkraut, schnaps, schnitzel, seltzer, smearcase, spaetzle, springerle, spritz, stein, stollen, streusel, strudel, tannenbaum, thuringer, torte, verboten, waltz, wanderlust, weinstube, weissbeer, weltanschauung, weltschmerz, wiener, wunderbar, wunderkind, wurst, yodel, zeitgeist, zigzag, and zwieback.

German loanwords also come into the American vocabulary not only by way of German-Americans, but also via advertising slogans, such as "Fahrvergnügen." Whith the latter, the use of a German word connotes quality, and is a marker indicating that the product is "Made in Germany." Another popular advertising gimmick is to add "fest" to any kind of possible sale. Thus, a sale in November becomes a November-Fest. Then, of course, there are the real festivals or celebrations, such as Oktoberfest.

German has been contributing to the molding and shaping of the language spoken in America. This is a result of the substantial German immigrations, and of the fact that German, historically, has been so widely spoken in the U.S.

Where is German spoken? Obviously most widely in the states and regions where the German-American element is predominant. The preservation of the German language was especially strong among those referred to as the church-Germans, for whom the church was a central institution in their lives and which used to place an emphasis on the German heritage. German has also usually more strongly maintained in rural communities, which tended to remain stable and constant for generations, and was usually close-knit. Finally, German tends to be spoken in two contexts: first, in the family, and second, within the framework of ethnic institutions and organizations.

Who speaks German? the majority of those who speak German are American-born, whose ancestors came anywhere from one to eight generations ago to America. Also, most have had no formal education with the German language, but have mainly been taught by members of their families.

The history of German as an ethnic language reaches back to the beginnings of German immigration. It has been spoken since 1608, when the first permanent German settlers arrived at Jamestown. The first recorded reference to a sermon having been presented in German dates to 1657 in New Amsterdam, which, of course, was heavily settled by Germans. Also, German was one of the official languages at New Sweden.

After the founding of Germantown in 1683, German flourished with the beginnings of ever-increasing waves of German immigration. In the 18th century, the question arose about establishing German as an official language.

During the American Revolution, the Continental Congress had numerous proclamations and broadsheets printed in German, beginning in 1774 with the proceedings of the Continental Congress. The Articles of Confederation of the Continental Congress also appeared in German, and many more publications were issued in German, clearly underscoring recognition of its importance.

At the same time, the German-language press had already been well established for several decades, the first German-language newspaper having been published in 1732 by Benjamin Franklin, the *Philadelphische Zeitung*. Also noteworthy is the fact that the first announcement of the Declaration of Independence appeared 5 July 1776 in Henry Miller's newspaper, the *Staatsbote*. In 1743, the

Germantown printer, Christoph Saur, had printed the first Bible in America in German.

The question often arises as to whether there was a vote to make German an official language on a national basis - the answer is that there almost was. In 1794, German-Americans from the state of Virginia petitioned the House of Representatives that U. S. laws be also printed in German. The Speaker of the House, Frederick Mühlenberg of Pennsylvania, was also president of the German Society of Pennsylvania, and desired very much to maintain his position in the House, which meant that he had to play politics.

At that time, there was a great deal of anti-immigrant sentiment rampant in the country, due to the French Revolution and the fear of "foreigners," i.e., non-Anglos. Rather than support the German-American petition, Mühlenberg referred it to a committee, which meant death by pocket veto. It was then re-submitted again, but again was tabled by referral to a committee, which was charged with investigating the matter. This petition was submitted at the same time when the question of the naturalization of immigrants was being discussed. Mühlenberg apparently must have felt that to support such a petition would have weakened not only his position as the House Speaker, but that of the naturalization legislation.

The myth which emerged from this was that German almost became a national language except for one vote by Mühlenerg, which of course was not the case. Even if it had been brought to a vote, German would not have been established as the official U. S. language, but as a co-equal with English in terms of printing laws, documents, etc.

As mentioned earlier, this had already been done during the American Revolution by the Continental Congress, so German already had been recognized as an executive language during the Revolution.

The one-vote-myth story most likely derives from what happened in Pennsylvania. In 1828, a motion was defeated by one vote to make German co-equal with English. However, it should be noted that many states recognized the importance of German, and authorized the printing of state documents in German, such as Ohio (1817).

In 1843, a Pennsylvania German representative in the House moved that the annual message be published in German, a motion which was defeated by three votes. An examination of where the votes came from was revealing. In the German Belt states, 55 were for and 5 against, in the non-German Belt states 31 for and 81 against. Hence, the voting clearly was on ethnic lines, with states with German-Americans voting for, and the predominantly Anglo states voting against.

In 1853, the *Congressional Globe* appeared in several issues in German. During the Civil War, there was another attempt made to have documents published in German. This motion passed in the Senate, but was defeated in the House, when a nativist Anglo-oriented representative stated: "I submit the question whether we are to have a national language or not." In this resulting vote, the New England and Atlantic states voted against, and the Midwestern states voted for it.

This was the last real attempt at the national level to petition for the publication of documents in German. However, numerous states did pass and retain regulations to print and publish documents in German. These remained in place until the time of World War I, when they were revoked.

By the time of the Civil War, German-Americans had begun to make the transition from their efforts at having documents printed and published in German to a more effective strategy at language maintenance and preservation - they moved for the establishment of bilingual educational programs. This was in private and public institutions. For public schools, the heyday for German bilingual instruction was from 1840 to 1918, when German instruction was eliminated or banned across the country. An example of this can be found in statistics for high school students of German. In 1915, 25% were enrolled in German, but in 1922 only .6% were. By 1978, 2.4% of high school students were enrolled in German, or approximately 10% of the number before the First World War. There is no question that the First World War had dealt the German language a crippling blow in terms of instructional programs.

The states where German instruction is strongest in terms of enrollment today tend to be those with large numbers of German-Americans, such as Pennsylvania, Illinois, and Ohio.

Not until 1923 was the ban on German instruction lifted. However, German instruction was re-introduced only in secondary schools, not in elementary and middle schools. As a reflection of the ethnic revival of the 1970s a number of German bilingual schools were re-established in Cincinnati, St. Louis, Milwaukee, Pittsburgh, and Chicago. Two all-German private schools were also established in Washington, D. C. and New York. By the 1980s, there were close to one hundred Saturday schools in various cities which offered German instruction. German is also taught in private and parochial schools, especially by the Catholic, Lutheran, and Mennonite Churches, as well as by various sectarian groups.

Clearly, German should be reintroduced at the elementary level, especially in those areas with a strong German heritage, as it is there where the interest is the greatest. As was the case in the 19th century, it is quite clear, however, that German will not be re-introduced unless German-Americans apply the appropriate pressure to have it re-instated.

There are other institutions which support the German language today, including German-language publications (ca. 50), German radio programs (ca. 175), churches with German services (ca. 2,000), as well as the numerous German-American societies.

Recent studies indicate that German is more widely spoken than is realized. In spite of two world wars, it is rather surprising how much survived the first half of the 20th century. This provides rich ground for the preservation and maintenance of the German language, especially in view of the ethnic revival in general and the interest in the German heritage in particular.

The historical importance of the German language to German-Americans was expressed in glowing terms by *Der Goldne Wegweiser* (*The Golden Signpost*) , which stated that German "is one of the oldest, purest, and most cultivated of the living languages and surpasses most modern languages in richness and strength, in malleability and suppleness. It must therefore be especially important to our German compatriots in America that their descendants also learn not merely to understand their beautiful native language without difficulty, but to know it thoroughly and to speak it." It noted that this certainly was "the most earnest wish of most of the citizens of this country who have immigrated from Germany."

History shows that successful language maintenance of an ethnic group has always been dependent upon the functioning of a network of support factors. The main components of the German-American network were: 1. thousands of German-American churches; 2. the parochial schools operated by the churches and the schools of the Turners and Freethinkers; 3. German instructional programs in the public schools, including bilingual education, as in Cincinnati; 4. the great variety of German Vereins (clubs) by both the Verein-Germans and the Church-Germans; 5. the relatively homogeneous ethnic neighborhood with restaurants, shops, and services; 6. the continued arrival of new immigrants; and 7. toleration, acceptance and integration in the U. S. body politic. Central to all these factors was the support group of the immediate family, and its interest in maintaining and preserving the German language.

Even with these support factors in place, a degree of language-shift was inevitable before the world wars due to the fact that English served as the official language of the U. S. However, it was the First World War which struck a devastating blow to the German language. Author Kurt Vonnegut captured his family's flight from German in this quote from his autobiographical *Palm Sunday*: ". . . the anti-Germanism in this country during the First World War so shamed and dismayed my parents that they resolved to raise me without acquainting me with the language or the literature or the music or the oral family histories which my ancestors had loved. They volunteered to make me ignorant and rootless as proof of their patriotism."

German, nonetheless, is still more widely spoken in the U. S. than is commonly realized, but the emphasis today has shifted to the re-discovery of German-American history and heritage. This in turn, may rekindle an interest in the German language.

22. Religious Influences

German-American communities have been defined in terms of their religious or secular institutions, so historians have spoken of the religious and secular parts of the community.

The religious element consisted of German-Americans who belonged to Protestant, Catholic, and Jewish religious institutions and organizations, which formed a central focal point of their religious and social lives. As a group, they have often been referred to as the church Germans, or *Kirchdendeutsche*. They established a wide variety of religious institutions, including hospitals, old peoples' homes, schools, seminaries, societies, and of course, places of worship. Many of them maintained German bookstores, where the publications of their own presses were available.

In religious educational institutions, German was an academic subject as well as the language of instruction. Some of these religious bodies held little in common with one another and went their own way in accordance with their own denomination, so they developed their own unique, religiously oriented social, educational, and sometimes even economic and political institutions. At times, the representatives of a particular religious denomination or the editor of the group's publications would engage in theological and doctrinal debates and disputes with other denominational publications.

Politically, the church Germans were conservative. Historically, some of them were staunchly anti-radical, anti-socialist, and especially anti-Forty-Eighter. Indeed, the latter were often viewed as divisive. However, most did not officially and overtly engage in political affairs and issues, except when there was an issue that directly affected their particular denomination, such as the issue of language instruction in parochial schools or abortion.

Religion and heritage were closely intertwined. Perhaps the most important institution for the preservation of the German language in America was the church. The church Germans used the German language and heritage to ward off heresy, maintain unity, prevent losses, and exclude external influences. This promoted a sense of a denomination's unique identity and religious particularity. Also, religiously oriented immigrants tended to come together in groups and stay together, and in such communities the church was the most important institution outside the family. Often in rural areas there would not even be a public school, for the only school in the area would be the parochial school.

Church Germans believed that language and faith were interrelated, so German was well maintained by the various religious denominations. Religion nurtured and was nurtured by religious consciousness. The least Anglicized communities were usually those with the strongest religious ties. Also, it is interesting to note that in German-American literature every author who was American-born and wrote in German came from a church-centered community. In fact, it is quite common for German-Americans of four or more generations to speak German, p articularly if they are from such a church-oriented background.

Such religious denominations were always youth oriented in terms of their educational programs and publications. Although a quite diverse group, their common bond was a commitment to the German heritage. It is estimated that there are still about two thousand congregations in the United States that hold German services, weekly, monthly, or annually. However, by the 1950s most German-American churches had made the language shift to English, mainly because of the desire to keep the youth within the fold. Although German-American denominations in the main have made the language shift, they clearly maintain a strong sense of identity as

German-American religious denominations, and many of them continue to sponsor occasional German services and hold German-style dinners as well as church festivals. Also, German-American church records are highly important for the study of German immigration and settlement history, as well as for the family history of congregational members.

It is beyond the scope of this work to provide a detailed discussion of individual denominations founded by German-Americans, but references to works dealing with them can be found in the bibliographical sources listed at the end of this volume.

IV: The German-American Experience

Drum steh'n wir stolz auf festem Grunde,
Den unsere Kraft der Wildnis nahm,
Wie war's mit eurem Staatenbunde,
Wenn nie zu euch ein Deutscher kam?
Und wie in Bürgerkriegstagen,
Ja schon beim ersten Freiheitsschrei:
Wir dürfen's unbestritten sage,
Da waren Deutsche auch dabei!

* * *

Thus, with great pride on this soil we stand,
Which from the wilds our strength brought claim,
Ever wonder then, what kind of land,
'twould be if n'er a German came?
And so we declared in Lincoln's day,
And that day freedom's horn first blew-
Yes, we dare undeniably say:
At your side there were Germans too!

Konrad Krez

23. The German-American Heritage

What began as a trickle of German emigration to America - a few settlers in Jamestown in 1608, a handful of Mennonite families in Pennsylvania in 1683 - gradually swelled into a tide over the next three centuries as eight million individuals from Germany and the German-speaking regions of Europe ventured across the ocean to the New World. Today, German-Americans can be found in every part of the U. S.

To honor the achievements, contributions, and history of this country's largest ethnic group, German-American Day was established by presidential proclamation in 1987. Celebrated annually on the 6th of October, this day sets aside a special time to explore the hardships, successes, traditions, and heritage of the German-American legacy.

It followed the successful celebration of the German-American Tricentennial in 1983, which was patterned after the traditional annual celebration of German Day on the 6th of October.

As Albert B. Faust stated at the 250th anniversary of Germantown's founding in 1933, German-Americans "have had their share of failure and success, of trial and triumph, of labor and honest effort in the building of the American nation. They are privileged to love and cherish America as rightful partners" with the other various groups which compose our multi-ethnic society. Faust rightfully noted that the study of German-American history "makes us better Americans, secure in traditions of service, true in devotion to national ideals."

Today, German-American Day is celebrated annually from coast to coast - an indication that the German-American legacy is one with roots reaching back to the 17th century, and one which has been and promises to be a permanent factor and dimension in American history and life. In 1989, the German-American Heritage Month, centered on German-American Day, was first celebrated in Cincinnati, and thereafter spread across the country

24. Coming to America

German immigrants journeyed across the Atlantic for a wide variety of reasons. Some were forced from their homelands because of religious or political persecution, others were driven away by crop failures or war, and a great many were simply lured by the promise of a better life.

Regardless of their motivations for coming to America, immigrants needed solid information to prepare for life in a new land. Although letters served as a primary source of knowledge about America, many people turned to emigrant guidebooks, or *Auswanderer-Ratgeber*, for additional facts on subjects that ranged from weights and measures to climate and soil quality.

At least 300 guidebooks were published, a few of which were scandalous deceptions, including one that duped naive readers with schemes for discovering gold in the uncharted regions of the New World. One of the most reliable emigrant guidebooks was published in 1851 by F. W. Bogen, a Boston minister. Bogen doled out travel tips, helpful addresses, and sage advice, much of which became part and parcel of the German-American *Weltanschauung*, or philosophy of life. In his book Bogen advised immigrants, "Let us be temperate, industrious, and frugal . . . let us build up in our hearts a temple, wherein the rational farseeing spirit of American liberty may live and flourish, and thus we may become good, happy, and free American citizens."

The majority of German immigrants arriving in America deliberately moved to areas where friends and relatives had already settled, places where the familiar faces and customs would help ease the adjustment of life in a strange country. The letters and reports sent back home from immigrants established many links between the

Old and New Worlds, and encouraged even more family members and neighbors to migrate to the same area.

This pattern of "chain migration" led to the development of entire German communities such as the Swiss-German town of New Glarus, Wisconsin, known for its Swiss architecture, cheese, and annual Wilhelm Tell festival, or Oldenburg, Indiana, which resembles a northern German village, right down to the street signs in German. Today, German-American communities retain traces of their founders' homelands through customs, dialects, and place names. Contacts between these New and Old World communities still exist, often in the form of sister-city relationships.

Many U. S. cities also share a common bond due to the chain migration that continued within America. Milwaukee, for example, was the first home of a large number of Pomeranians who later settled at German Lake, Minnesota. Cincinnati is historically intertwined with the towns of New Ulm, Minnesota and Guttenberg, Iowa, where the architecture clearly reveals the influence of Cincinnati styles. The German Settlement Society of Philadelphia founded Hermann, Missouri, a town still renowned for its German influenced architecture and fine wines, as well as its outstanding museum, the Deutschheim State Historic Site.

25. Home Away From Home

In the early 19th century, ambitious chain migration efforts were undertaken to establish German-American populated states in Wisconsin, Missouri, and Texas. While there was some success in concentrating a large number of German immigrants in these areas, the lack of support from a unified nation-state abroad kept the dream of a "New Germany" from actually materializing, although these efforts did result in large concentrations of German immigrants in the aforementioned states, as well as elsewhere.

Most successful at preserving the language and culture were the many German-founded communities or city districts that flourished into thriving centers of agriculture, trade and industry. These so-called "Little Germanies" became the hubs of German-American social, business, and political life. Stores stocked German books and specialty foods, theater staged the plays of Goethe and Schiller, and clubhouses thronged with rifle, athletic, and choral societies. People were kept abreast of local issues through publicly posted German-language newspapers, and beer halls became popular gathering spots for games, celebrations, and community meetings.

Almost every large city had its "Little Germany," some being more influential than others. Milwaukee's large and unified German community, for instance, not only enjoyed firmly established economic and cultural roots, but carried political clout in the city government as well. In Cincinnati, German immigration peaked in the late 1800s, setting the stage for a political presence that lasted well into this century. Even as early as 1840, Cincinnati, practically declared itself bilingual by establishing German classes in the public schools and expending a substantial portion of the library budget on German books.

118

Despite German immigrants' efforts to recreate aspects of their homeland, their communities were not isolated islands untainted by the outside world. Occasionally, other groups viewed these German enclaves with disfavor, and even Benjamin Franklin, fearing that the English-founded Pennsylvania would be overrun by foreigners, disdainfully asked, "Why should the Palatine boors be suffered . . . (to) establish their language and customs to the exclusion of ours?"

Eventually, American ideals and manners did permeate German communities, contributing to the growth and development of a German-American synthesis of the Old and the New Worlds, which found expression in the many German-American societies, schools, traditions, and celebrations that had taken root.

26. The Anti-German Hysteria

In spite of their many contributions to the building of this nation, including innovations in technology, agriculture, education, and the arts, which gave us such everyday staples as the Linotype machine, kindergarten, and the Brooklyn Bridge, Steinway pianos, and blue jeans, German-Americans became the targets of an Anti-German Hysteria during the era of World War I.

Almost every state and community had a "Security League," "Citizen's Patriotic League," or some type of volunteer vigilante group that attacked anything German in their area. Increasingly, all things German were eliminated or shunned - street names were altered, books were burned, theaters were closed, and the German language was banned by state councils from schools, churches, telephone conversations, and semi-public places.

Overly zealous patriots smeared the homes of German-Americans with yellow paint, or forced German-Americans to kiss the flag on their knees to prove their loyalty to America. In an attempt to avoid persecution, many German-American businesses, societies, and individuals anglicized their names. Altogether, 6,300 German-Americans were interned as a result of the anti-Germanism of the time, thus establishing a model for more large scale internment programs during the Second World War.

Reaching a fever pitch, this Anti-German Hysteria occasionally led to mob violence and even murder. The first well-known case of a lynching of a German-American took place on 5 April 1918 in Collinsville, Illinois, where Robert Prager was strung up by a mob solely on the basis of his ethnicity. President Wilson's failure to respond immediately and condemn this violent act only served to encourage further prejudice, resulting in additional boycotts of German-American businesses and newspapers.

By the end of the First World War, 37 states had enacted legislation against foreign-language instruction, among them 26 states with explicit prohibitions against the German language. The German language itself was considered a language that "disseminates the ideals of autocracy, brutality, and hatred" - in the words of one California school official. Some school districts were not content with banning German, but also held ceremonies to burn German textbooks.

German-Americans continued to suffer ethnic intimidation and harassment during World War II, when more than 10,000 innocent German-Americans were interned in concentration camps. Even after the war, ethnic slurs prevailed as the media and large segments of the American public continued to label German-Americans as "Krauts" or "Nazis." Not surprisingly, German-Americans opted for a "submerged ethnicity," limiting the celebration of their heritage to the closed spaces of family, church, and cultural organizations, many of which were screened by the FBI.

No official apologies for the wrongs and injustices suffered by German-Americans during the world wars has ever been issued, although this has been for the Japanese-Americans.

From 1941 to 1951, there were almost no major German-festivities held and to avoid public abuse, people would only cautiously identify themselves as "Americans of German descent," rather than as "German-Americans."

27. A Revival of Ethnic Pride

In the 1950s, the glacial attitude toward German-Americans began to thaw as Germany emerged as a powerful NATO ally. Encouraged by the fading of war-engendered animosities, German-American organizations again celebrated their ethnic heritage by reviving traditional festivals, which, apart from raising funds and showcasing customs, built bridges between cultures. While the increasingly popular Oktoberfest and other celebrations of food, drink and song may have played into Gemütlichkeit stereotypes, these, were exactly the kinds of positive images needed to contrast with the negative ones that lingered after the wars. Also important were the Steuben Parades in New York, Philadelphia, and Chicago, which became major public expressions of German-American heritage.

An additional boost to ethnic identification came in the '60s and '70s with the increased national interest in "roots," which helped to generate the widespread acceptance and recognition of ethnicity as a permanent and vital factor in American life. In the wake of this new trend, the Society for German-American Studies was formed in 1968, establishing the areas of German-American history, literature, and culture as legitimate academic fields.

The celebration of the American Bicentennial in 1976 proved to be a genuine turning-point in German-American history, as it served to illuminate the role that German-Americans had played in the building of the nation for the first time since before the period of the world wars. This was accomplished by conferences, symposia, exhibits, publications, etc.

It was virtually re-discovered that apart from Baron von Steuben, who had trained American troops during the Revolution and is honored every year with parades in New York, Philadelphia, and

Chicago, entire regiments of German-Americans had fought in the Revolution, and Washington's very own private bodyguard had been an all-German unit, the Independent Troop of the Horse.

The Bicentennial, hence, served as the occasion, whereby not only the role German-Americans had played in the Revolution, but in American history in general was re-discovered. At the academic level, German-American Studies further developed, while in American society at large, a sense of pride in the German heritage emerged.

Among those who have played an important role since the time of the American Bicentennial representing German-American affairs nationally, the following stand forth: Ilse Hoffmann (Steuben Society of America), Helmut Krueger (United German-American Committee), Ernst Ott (German-American National Congress), William Hetzler (German-American Steuben Parade Committee), and Don Heinrich Tolzmann (Solciety for German-American Studies).

In 1980, the U.S. Census statistically established German-Americans as the largest ethnic group in America. Soon after, the 1983 German-American Tricentennial commemorated the founding of the first permanent German settlement at Germantown, Pennsylvania, rejuvenating older German-American organizations and inspiring new ones. The Tricentennial centered around the 6th of October, the date on which Germantown was founded in 1683, and the traditional day that German Day was celebrated before the world wars.

In 1986, German-American societies, churches, and publications launched a national campaign, initiated by the Society for German-American Studies, to pass a Congressional resolution declaring the 6th of October as an annual "German-American Day." With the strong support of the German-American National Congress, the

Steuben Society of America, and the United German-American Committee, German-Americans attained their goal. The congressional resolution became law on 2 October 1987, when President Ronald Reagan signed the proclamation in a special Rose Garden ceremony, symbolically restoring the place of German-Americans in the American mosaic. President Reagan's proclamation stated as follows that:

"More Americans trace their heritage back to German ancestry than any other nationality. More than seven million Germans have come to our shores through the years and today some 60 million Americans one in four - are of German descent. Few people have blended so completely into the multicultural tapestry of American society and yet have made such singular economic, political, social, scientific, and cultural contributions to the growth and success of these United States as have Americans of German extraction.

The United States has embraced a vast array of German traditions, institutions, and influences. Many of these have become so accepted as parts of our way of life that their ethnic origin has been obscured. For instance, Christmas trees and Broadway musicals are familiar features of American society. Our kindergartens, graduate schools, the social security system, and labor unions are all based on models derived from Germany.

German teachers, musicians, and enthusiastic amateurs have left an indelible imprint on classical music, hymns, choral singing, and marching bands in our country. In architecture and design, German contributions include the modern suspension bridge, Bauhaus, and Jugenstil. German-American scientists have helped make the United States the world's pioneer in research and technology.

The American work ethic, a major factor in the rapid rise of the United States to preeminence in agriculture and industry, owes much to German-Americans' commitment to excellence.

For more than three centuries, Germans have helped build, invigorate, and strengthen this country. But the United States has given as well as received. Just a generation ago, America conceived of and swiftly implemented the Marshall Plan, Europe. The Berlin Airlift demonstrated the American commitment to the defense of freedom when, still recovering from war, Berlin was threatened by strangulation from the Soviets.

Today, the Federal Republic of Germany is a bulwark of democracy in the heart of a divided Europe. Germans and Americans are rightfully proud of our shared heritage. For more than three decades the German-American partnership has been a linchpin in the Western Alliance. Thanks to it, a whole generation of Americans and Europeans has grown up free to enjoy the fruits of liberty.

Our histories are thus intertwined. We now contribute to each other's trade, enjoy each other's cultures, and learn from each other's experiences. The German-American Friendship Garden, which will soon be dedicated in the District of Columbia in the near future, is symbolic of the close and amicable relationships between West Germany and the United States."

The President then noted that Congress, by Public Law 100-104, had designated the 6th of October 1987 as German-American Day, and urged everyone to learn more about the contributions German-Americans have made "to the life and culture of the United States and to observe this day with appropriate ceremonies and activities." Since that time German-American Day has become an annual day of commemoration, which is celebrated from coast to coast.

In 1989, the first German-American Heritage Month was launched in Cincinnati, Ohio Centered on German-American Day, this provided the opportunity for a month-long program of lectures, exhibits, celebrations, and festivities dealing with German-American history.

On 5 April 1993, Prager Memorial Day was held in remembrance of all those who suffered under the anti-German hysteria and sentiment of the world wars. It was named in honor of Robert Paul Prager who was lynched in Collinsville, Illinois in 1918 during the Anti-German Hysteria of World War I, and was held on the 75th anniversary of his lynching. In remembrance of this dark chapter in American history, an Ohio Historical Marker entitled "Anti-German Hysteria" was dedicated in Cincinnati, Ohio in the same year, and is located in Fairview Park overlooking the town's old German district, the Over-the-Rhine district.

In 1997, a historical marked was dedicated at Jamestown, Virginia in honor of the arrival of the first Germans in America on 1 October 1608. This was due to the work of the German Heritage Society of Greater Washington, D.C.

This brought international attention not only to the role German-Americans have played in American history in general, but to the fact that they had been present at the very beginnings of American history.

1997 also marked the 100th anniversary of the Hermann Monument at New Ulm, Minnesota, at which time it was declared a national monument and symbol of the German-American heritage. Patterned after the Hermann Monument in Detmold, Germany, the German-American monument signified the German-American experience: from the demanding struggle of the immigration to establishing a new life in America. For German-Americans, in general the monument signified the pride in the German heritage, as well as in German-American contributions to building and preserving the U. S. Hermann also signified something of the fighting spirit necessary to preserve and maintain the German heritage in the future.

In 1998, the 150th anniversary of the German Revolution of 1848 was celebrated and was particularly commemorated in the U. S. through the annual meeting and symposium of the Society for German-American Studies, which was held at Indianapolis, Indiana.

28. German-Americans Today

Today, German-Americans reside in every state of the Union. In rural areas, German-Americans still live and work on the same land that their families settled during the 19th century. In fact, many farms have been passed down from generation to generation since colonial times, revealing high value placed on land ownership in German-American families. The majority of urban-dwelling German-Americans, however, moved to the suburbs during the postwar era, as inner cities began to decay. As a result, urban German communities are no longer geographically defined by neighborhoods as in the past century, but are now held together by cultural organizations.

The re-emergence of pride in German-American heritage has taken place in modest steps over the span of many years. Heritage societies continue to blossom across the U. S. and new interests in German history and language have taken root, as have efforts to address the injustice of the past.

All of the events and activities since the 1960s signify a coming together of German-Americans, and are best symbolized by German-American Day. Paying tribute to the German heritage and the multifaceted relationship between German-speaking countries and America, this day honors the achievements of the millions of German-speaking immigrants and their descendants, who continue to explore and express what it means to be German-American today.

Although German-American identity means different things to different people, most would probably agree with the definition of Carl Schurz, who advised German-Americans to "adopt the best parts of the American Spirit and melt these with the best parts of the German Spirit."

Kuno Francke, a professor of German at Harvard University, has described German-Americans as the heirs and guardians of the German heritage in America, and in so doing provided some sound advice with regard to the preservation thereof.

He advised that German-Americans should each in their own individual way cultivate the German heritage: "Let us, like Carl Schurz, take our stand by the side of our fellow citizens of other descent as fully rounded personalities, bent on high achievements; let us take prominent part in all matters concerning the political, intellectual, moral, social, and artistic elevation of the masses . . . in other words, let us make the best of German culture in the service and for the benefit of our new fatherland."

He further advised that German-Americans should not abdicate their rights, but insist on the cessation of any and all encroachments or injustices pertaining to the German heritage. Moreover, they should do their best to provide for a fuller understanding and sympathy for the German-speaking countries in the American press, in the institutions of learning, and among the American public in general.

Today, the German-American heritage is, as Schurz observed, a blending of the Old and the New Worlds. So much of the German heritage has become part of everyday life that many are not even aware of the German origins, as so much of it has become a basic part of the very fabric of American life.

The Germans who have been coming to America since 1608 have clearly impressed a distinctly German flavor on the development of the U. S., which has enriched the country and has shaped and deeply influenced the American way of life. This has led to the observation that if you scratch the surface on just about any aspect of American life, chances are that you might come upon German origins.

At the threshold of the 21st century, German-Americans can look back on four centuries of American life, as well as look forward to the celebration of the German-American Quadricentennial in 2008.

Obviously, an ethnic element as large as that constituted by the German-Americans is destined to continue to play an important role in the nation's social, cultural, economic, and political life, as it has in the past. In conclusion, it can be reiterated that German-Americans have played a decisive role in the history of the growth and development of the U. S., and that as one-fourth of the population they certainly merit consideration when it comes to national, state, and local history.

The answer to the question posed by the German-American author, Konrad Krez, "Ever wonder, then, what kind of land, 'twould be if n'er a German came?" is quite simple: The U. S. would have turned out to be an entirely different country than it is today.

V. Appendix: The German American Heritage Month

Adopt the best parts of the American Spirit,
and melt these with the best parts of the German Spirit!

Carl Schurz

It is essential that we ourselves ever bear in mind
and guard as our heritage, the spiritual and material
contributions of our German ancestors
to American life, culture and progress,
especially in the fields of literature, art, and science,
in order that they be recognized
on the pages of history in the future.

H. A. Rattermann

This month centers on German-American Day, the 6th of October, the date on which Germantown, Pennsylvania was founded in 1683. It begins in mid-September and goes through mid-October, and provides the opportunity to include all German-American related events into a month-long program. The purpose of the month is to illuminate the role German-Americans have played in American history, and make this known to the general public.

The German-American Heritage Month includes German-American festivities, such as Oktoberfest, but also lectures, exhibits, films, etc. Special proclamations should be requested from local and regional authorities, which highlight the German heritage of the region. If the German-American Heritage Month is currently not celebrated locally, then a planning committee can be organized, so that it can be introduced.

Also, plans should be made for the celebration of the 400th anniversary of the arrival of the first Germans in America at Jamestown in the year 2008. This should become a central part of planning and programming for the annual German-American Heritage Month. Thereafter, anniversaries can also be planned, such as the 410th in 2018, the 425th in 2033, etc. There are also other related kinds of programming that should be taken into consideration with regard to the annual German-American Heritage Month.

Inquiries should be made as to whether German-American history and heritage are included in the educational curricula of area schools, colleges, and universities. If they are not included, the reference should be made to the U. S. Census statistics, found elsewhere in this volume, and mention made as to the statistical importance of the German-American element. On this basis, the request should be made that German-American Studies be included in instructional programming.

Inquiries should also be made as to whether German instruction is being offered in the schools. If it is not currently being offered, then the suggestion should be made that it would be advisable to do so given the population of German heritage. It should also be recommended that the German-American Heritage Month become part of the annual calendar of the area schools.

In is also important to check the holdings of area libraries to ascertain what kinds of materials they have regarding German-American history. The selective bibliography included in this volume can be utilized as a guide to sources. If libraries do not have such materials, then the request can be made that such materials be placed on order. Moreover, it can be suggested that they be placed on display during the German-American Heritage Month.

State and local historical and genealogical societies may also have resources and programs pertaining to German-American history and heritage. Inquiries can be undertaken as well as to their program offerings and sources in this area, and if nothing is available, then suggestions can be made that they include consideration of the German-American dimension. They also could become involved in the German-American Heritage Month, and this recommendation should also be made.

Find out what local and state organizations are available, and contact them with regard to involvement and participation in the German-American Heritage Month.

If there are German-American societies in your area, become involved in them, and suggest that they address some of the suggestions discussed here. If there are no such societies, find out who might be interested in one, and call for an organizational meeting, so that one can be organized. Such an organization can take as its focal point the planning and organization of the annual German-American Heritage Month.

The selective bibliography in this work can be consulted for further information on German-American history and culture. In these sources further information can be found with regard to a variety of aspects of German-American experience.

Up-to-date information on the field of German-American Studies can be obtained from the Society for German-American Studies, which publishes a quarterly newsletter, the *Yearbook of German-American Studies*, and sponsors annual meetings and symposia.

VI. Select Bibliography

1. Bibliographical Sources:

Arndt, Karl J. R. and May E. Olson. *The German-Language Press of the Americas* 3 vols. (München: K. G. Saur, 1976-80).

Krewson, Margrit B. *Immigrants from the German-Speaking Countries of Europe: A Selective Bibliography of Reference Works.* (Washington, D. C.: Library of Congress, 1991).

Pochmann, Henry August. *Bibliography of German Culture in America to 1940.* (Millwood, NY: Kraus, 1982).

Schultz, Arthur R. *German-American Relations and German Culture in America: A Subject Bibliography, 1941-1980.* (Millwood, NY: Kraus, 1984).

Tolzmann, Don Heinrich, ed. *Americana Germanica: Paul Ben Baginsky's Bibliography of German Works Relating to America, 1493-1800.* (Bowie, MD: Heritage Books, Inc., 1995)

_____. *Catalog of the German-Americana Collection, University of Cincinnati.* (München: K. G. Saur, 1990).

_____. *German-Americana: A Bibliography.* (Metuchen, NJ: Scarecrow Pr., 1975).

Ward, Robert E, *A Bio-Bibliography of German-American Writers, 1670-1970.* (White Plains, NY: Kraus International Publications, 1985).

2. Biographical Sources:

Haller, Charles., *Distinguished German-Americans* (Bowie, MD: Heritage Books, Inc., 1995).

140

Tolzmann, Don Heinrich, *German-American Biographical Index CDROM*. (Bowie, MD: Heritage Books, Inc., 1999).

_____. *Ohio Valley German Biographical Index*. (Bowie, MD: Heritage Books, Inc., 1992).

_____. *Ohio Valley German Biographical Index: A Supplement*. (Bowie, MD: Heritage Books, Inc., 1993).

_____. *Upper Midwest German Biographical Index*. (Bowie, MD: Heritage Books, Inc., 1993).

Wilk, Gerard, *Americans from Germany*. Edited by Don Heinrich Tolzmann. (Indianapolis: Max Kade German-American Center & Indiana German Heritage Society, 1995).

3. Genealogical Sources:

Bahlow, Hans, *Dictionary of German Names,* Translated by Edda Gentry. (Madison: Max Kade Institute for German-American Studies, 1993).

Baxter, Angus. *In Search of your German Roots: A Complete Guide to Tracing Your Ancestors in the Germanic Areas of Europe*. (Baltimore: Genealogical Pub. Co., 1994).

Jones, George F., *German-American Names*, 2nd ed. (Baltimore: Genealogical Pub. Col, 1995).

Thode, Ernest, *Address Book for Germanic Genealogy*, 2nd Rev. Ed. (Baltimore: Genealogical Pub. Co., 1983).

4. General Works:

Adams, Willi Paul. *The German-Americans: An Ethnic Experience*. Translated and adapted by LaVern J. Rippley and Eberhard

Reichmann. (Indianapolis: Max Kade German-American Center, Indiana University-Purdue University at Indianapolis, 1993).

Cazden, Robert E., *A Social History of the German Book Trade in America to the Civil War.* (Columbia, SC: Camden House, 1984).

Conzen, Kathleen Neils. "The Germans," in *Harvard Encyclopedia of American Ethnic Groups.* Stephen Thernstrom, ed. (Cambridge: Harvard University Pr., 1980), pp. 406-25.

Erhardt, Jacob, ed. *Adventures of a Greenhorn: An Autobiographical Novel by Robert Reitzel.* New German-American Studies, Vol. 3. (New York: Peter Lang Pub. Co., 1992).

Faust, Albert B., *The German Element in the U. S.* (New York: Steuben Society of America, 1927).

Geitz, Henry, ed. *The German-American Press.* (Madison: Max Kade Institute at the University of Wisconsin, 1992).

Greene, George Washington, *The German Element in the War for American Independence.* (Bowie, MD: Heritage Books, Inc., 1997).

Hoobler, Dorothy and Thomas. *The German-American Family Album.* (New York: Oxford University Pr., 1996).

Kamphoefner, Walter D. et al. *News from the Land of Freedom: German Immigrants Write Home.* (Ithaca: Cornell University Pr., 1991).

Lachner, Bert, ed., *Heimat North America.* (Chicago: Landmark Books, 1997).

Leubke, Frederick, *Germans in the New World: Essays in the History of Immigration.* (Urbana: University of Illinois Pr., 1990).

Merrill, Peter C., *German Immigrant Artists in America: A Biographical Dictionary*. (Metuchen, NJ: Scarecrow Press, 1997).

Moltmann, Günter, ed., *Germans to America: 300 Years of Immigration, 1683-1983*. (Stuttgart: Institute for Cultural Relations, 1983).

Ott, Franziska C., *Cincinnati German Imprints: A Checklist*. New German-American Studies, Vol. 7. (New York: Peter Lang Pub. Co., 1993).

Reichmann, Eberhard, *Hoosier German Tales - Small & Tall*. (Indianapolis: Max Kade German-American Center & Indiana German Heritage Society, 1991).

Reichmann, Eberhard et al, eds., *Emigration and Settlement Patterns of German Communities in North America*. (Indianapolis: Max Kade German-American Center & Indiana German Heritage Society, 1995).

Rippley, La Vern J., *The German-Americans*. (Lanham, MD: University Press of America, 1984).

Salmons, Joseph C., ed., *The German Language in America, 1683-1991*. (Madison: Max Kade German-American Institute, 1993).

Stuecher, Dorothea, *Twice Removed: The Experience of German-American Women Writers in the Nineteenth Century*. New German-American Studies, Vol. 1. (New York: Peter Lang Pub. Co., 1990).

Thomson, Colin D. and Charlotte Lang Brancaforte, eds. *The Golden Signpost: A Guide to Happiness and Prosperity*. (Madison: Max Kade Institute for German American Studies, University of Wisconsin-Madison, 1993).

Tolzmann, Don Heinrich, ed., *The German-American Experience*. (New York: Humanity Books, 2000).

Toth, Carolyn C., *German-English Bilingual Schools in America: The Cincinnati Tradition in Historical Context*. New German-American Studies, Vol. 2 (New York: Peter Lang Pub. Co., 1990).

Totten, Christine M., *Roots in the Rhineland: America's German Heritage in Three Hundred Years of Immigration, 1683-1983*. (New York: German Information Center, 1988).

Trommler, Frank and Joseph McVeigh, eds., *America and the Germans: An Assessment of a Three-Hundred-Year History*. 2 vols. (Philadelphia: University of Pennsylvania Pr., 1985).

Wittke, Carl, *The German-Language Press in America*. (Lexington: University of Kentucky Pr., 1957).

_____. *Refugees of Revolution: The German Forty-Eighters in America*. (Philadelphia: University of Pennsylvania, 1952).

5. Internet Sites:

German-Americana Collection at the University of Cincinnati
http://www.archives.uc.edu/german

German American Day
http:///www3.serve.com/shea/germusa/usafrg.htm

German American History and Heritage
http://www.germanheritage.com

Germans in America—Chronology (Library of Congress)
http://www.loc.gov/rr/european/imde/germchro.html

About the Author

Dr. Don Heinrich Tolzmann is recognized as "Father of German-American Day," the now official and annual celebration that honors the contributions of German-Americans to American life and culture. In 1989, he organized the first German-American Heritage Month centered on German-American Day. As Curator of the German-Americana Collection and Director of German-American Studies at the University of Cincinnati, he has led the movement to create a national and international awareness of the important but for so long neglected role played by German-Americans in the development of the American way of life. He is the author and editor of numerous books dealing with German-American history, literature and culture.

He edits a monographic series (*New German-American Studies*), has served as Ohio editor of the *New Yorker Staats-Zeitung*, editor of the *Zeitschrift für deutschamerikanische Literatur,* and on the editorial board of the *Yearbook for German-American Studies.* As an active, dedicated and informed member of most regional and national German-American organizations, he has frequently been called upon to represent German-American interests to the administrations in Washington, D.C.

He is the recipient of the Friendship Award of the Federal Republic of Germany as well as that country's Federal Cross of Merit (*Bundesverdienstkreuz*); the Ohioana Book Award, the Ficken Award from Baldwin-Wallace University; and the German-American of the Year Award from the Federation of German-American Societies. In addition, he has served for many years as President of the Society for German-American Studies. By promoting the development of teaching units for use in Ohio's schools and strengthening academic and personal ties between

Germany and the U. S., Dr. Tolzmann has performed exemplary service in raising community, state and regional awareness of the many contributions to American society made by German-Americans.

Index

Agassiz, Louis 57
Ammann 56
Anheuser-Busch 61
Anschuetz, Georg 58
Ascher, Carol 94
Autelmann 57
Bach 60, 75
Bancroft 69
Bancroft, Frederic 83
Bartholdt, Richard 50, 88
Barton, Benjamin Smith 68
Baum, L. Frank 94
Beck, Carl 71
Beethoven 75
Behr 60
Behrent, Georg 60
Beicken, Peter 94
Beissel, Johann Conrad 93
Bensinger, William 47
Berger, Thomas 94
Bierstadt, Albert 77
Bismarck, Otto von 12
Bitter, Karl 78
Blatz 61
Blickensderfer 57
Bloch, Felix 57
Bodmer, Karl 77
Boeing, William 56
Bogen, F. W. 115
Bolzius 24

148

Borein, Edward 78
Braeden, Eric 82
Brahm, John 81
Brahms 75
Braun, Wernher von 6, 57
Brill, John 58
Buchholz, Horst 81
Buck, Pearl S. 94
Buffalo Bill 77
Bukowski, Charles 94
Buschbek 46
Butz, Caspar 93
Carnegie, Andrew 58
Carsten-Miller, Ingeborg 94
Chrysler, Walter Percy 58
Claus, Santa 80
Cleveland, Grover 84
Cogswell 69
Columbus 15
Cooper 94
Coors 61
Cornwallis 39
Cosby, William 90
Cousin, Victor 68
Cramp, Charles 59
Cronau, Rudolf 22, 43
Custer, George Armstrong 21, 46
Dalfinger, Ambrosius 16
Damrosch, Leopold 74
Dehn, Adolf 78
Dicks, Rudi 80

Dietrich, Marlene 81
Dilger 46
Dirksen, Everett 85
Dock, Christopher 67
Dreiser, Theodore 93, 94
Drescher, Martin 93
Drumm, Georg 75
Duesenberg 58
Eggenhoffer, Nick 78
Ehrmann, Max 94
Eisenhower, Dwight D. 49, 75, 84
Emmerich, Charles 71
Entenmann 61
Faber, Eberhard 60
Faust, Albert B. 113
Federmann, Nikolaus 16
Fick, H. H. 70, 93
Fillmore, President 79
Fink, Albert 56
Fischer 58
Follen, Carl 68, 71
Francke, August Hermann 67
Francke, Kuno 128
Franklin, Benjamin 68, 89, 99, 118
Frick, Henry 58
Friebert, Stuart 94
Fritz, John 58
Froebel, Friedrich 70
Gates, General 40
Geisel, Theodore S. 94
Gemuender, Georg 59

Gericke, Wilhelm 74
Goethe . . . . vi, 117
Grant, President 84
Graupner, Johann 73, 74
Greene, General 39, 41
Griscom, John 69
Gronau 24
Gropius, Walter 79
Gunther, John 94
Haendel 75
Haller, Charles 82
Hamilton, Alexander 90
Haupt, Herman 56
Havemeyer, William 61
Haydn, Handel 73, 75
Hayes, President 84
Heilmann 61
Heinz, G. L. 60, 79
Heldreich Farghar, Norman von 49
Hellmann 61
Henke, William 49
Henried, Paul 81
Herbart, Johann Friedrich 69
Herchheimer, Nicholas 40
Hergesheimer, Joseph 94
Herkimer, Nicholas 40
Hermann, Monument 125
Hershey 61
Hetzler, William 122
Hinsdale, Burke 69
Hoffmann, Ilse 122

Hoffmann, Ilse 122
Hohermuth, Georg 16
Hoover, Herbert 84
Hudepohl 61
Hunt, Irmgard Elsner 93
Irving 94
Jaegers, Albert 78
Jahn, Friedrich Ludwig 71
Jahn, Helmut 79
Jefferson, Thomas 69
Jordan, Prof. 70
Juergens, Curt 81
Kade, Max 61, 72
Kahn, Lisa 94
Kalb, Heinrich de 40
Kalb, Johann de 40
Kapellhoff Day, Doris 81
Karl V 16
Kautz, August 49
Kautz, Major-General 45
Kempff, Louis 49
Keppler, Joseph 80
Kleinschmidt, Edward 56
Klemperer, Otto 74
Klemperer, Werner 82
Knabe 60
Knortz, Karl 93
Koerner, William Henry 78
Kollbrunner, Otto Oscar 93
Kraft 61
Kranich 60

Krapf, Norbert 94

Kreisler, Fritz 74

Kresge, Sebastian 60

Krez, Konrad . . . . ix, 3, 37, 54, 93, 111, 129

Kroger 61

Krueger, Helmut 122

Krueger, Walter 49

Küster, Arnold 21, 46

Laemmle, Carl 81

Lang, Fritz 81

Lauchheimer, Major 49

Lee, Robert E. 47

Lehmann, Lotte 74

Leisler, Jacob 17-19, 83

Leopold, Archbishop 24

Leutze, Emanuel 77

Lewisohn, Ludwig 94

Lieber, Francis 71

Lincoln, Abraham 83

Lincoln, President 80

Longfellow 68, 94

Lorre, Peter 81

Ludwig, Christopher 40-42

Luken, Thomas 85

Lutterloh, Heinrich 42

Mahler 75

Mann, Horace 68, 69

Mann, Thomas 93

Marix, Captain 49

Masur, Kurt 74

Mather, Cotton 67

Melville 94
Mencken, H. L. 94, 97
Mercator, Gerhard Kramer 15
Mergenthaler, Ottmar 59
Merrill, Peter 78
Metternich, Prince 11
Meyer, Oscar 61
Meyers, Captain 49
Milborne 19
Miller 61
Miller, Alfred Jacob 77
Miller, Henry 99
Miller, Joaquin 94
Minuit, Peter 17, 18, 83
Mozart 75
Mueller 61
Mueller, Lisel 94
Mühlenberg, Frederick 40, 100
Mühlenberg, Peter 39, 40, 78
Napoleon 10-12
Nast, Thomas 80
Neuharth, Allen 91
Nicholson, Gov. 18
Niers, Gert 93
Nies, Konrad 93
Nimitz, Chester 49
Nordhoff, Charles 94
Ochs, Adolph 91
Oglethorpe, General 24
Osterhaus, Major-general 45, 46
Ott, Ernst 122

Ottendorff, Nicholas von 39
Pabisch, Peter 93
Pabst 61
Pastorius, Franz Daniel 21, 67, 83, 93
Paur, Emil 74
Pelz 79
Penn, William 21
Pershing, John 49
Pestalozzi 69
Pitcher, Molly 78
Playel 60
Pochmann, Henry A. 95
Poe 94
Prager, Robert 119, 125
Prechter, Heinz 58
Pulitzer, Joseph 90
Rattermann, Heinrich A. 93
Reagan, President Ronald 123
Reck, Baron von 24
Redenbacher 61
Reiner, Fritz 74
Reiss, Winold 78
Reitzel, Robert 93
Richards, Henry Melchior Muhlenberg 42
Richter, Conrad 94
Rickenbacker, Eddie 49
Ridder 91
Ringler, F. A. 59
Rittenhouse, Wilhelm 60
Roebling, Don 49
Roebling, Johann August 49, 55, 56

Rohe, Mies van der 79
Rudolf, Max 74
Rungius, Carl 78
Rush, Benjamin 29
Salomon, Major-General 45
Saur, Christoph 22, 89, 100
Saxe, John Godfrey 94
Scharpenberg, Margot 94
Scheffauer, George 94
Schell 82
Schell, Maximillian 82
Schley, Winfield 49
Schlitz 61
Schnabel 60
Schnauber, Cornelius 81
Schneider, Charles 56
Schoen, Charles 58
Schott, John Paul 39
Schreyvogel, Charles 77
Schubert 75
Schultz, Charles 80
Schumacher, Ferdinand 60
Schumann 75
Schumann-Heink, Ernestine 74
Schurz, Carl 6, 78, 83, 84, 90, 127, 128, 133
Schurz, Major-General 45, 46
Schurz, Mrs. Carl 70
Schwab, Charles 58
Schwalbe, Lt. 49
Schwarzenegger, Arnold 61, 82
Schwarzkopf, Elisabeth 74

Schwarzkopf, Norman 50
Schweizer, J. Otto 78
Seidl, Anton 74
Seltzer, Olaf 77
Seuss, Dr. 94
Shaefer 61
Sherman 46
Siegel-Cooper 60
Sigel, Franz 78
Sigel, Major-General 45
Sirk, Douglas 81
Slezak, Walter 81
Sloughter, Col. 19
Smith, John 19
Smithmeyer 79
Sohmer 60
Sommer, Elke 81
Sousa, John Phillip 74
Spaatz, Carl 49
Spotswood, Gov. 58
Spreckels, Claus 60
Stahel, Major-General 45
Steck 60
Steiff, Margarete 64
Stein, Gertrude 94
Steinberg, William 74
Steiner, Max 82
Steiner, Ulrich 78
Steinmetz, Charles 56
Steinway 119
Steinway, Henry 60

Steinwehr, Major-General 45, 46
Sternberg, Josef von 81
Steuben, Friedrich Wilhelm von, ... 6, 41, 42, 78, 121
Stieglitz, Alfred 79
Stigel, Baron 57
Stowe, Calvin 68
Stowe, Harriet Beecher 68
Strauss 75
Strauss, Joseph 56
Stroh 61
Stroheim, Erich von 81
Studebaker 58
Stuhlinger, Ernst 57
Suckow, Ruth 94
Sumner, Charles 47
Sutro, Adolf 56
Sutter, John 57
Taylor, Bayard 94
Tell, Wilhelm 116
Thomas, Theodor 74
Thoreau 94
Ticknor 68
Timrod, Henry 94
Tolzmann, Don Heinrich 122, 145, 146
Trollope 63
Twain 94
Ulmer, Edgar 81
Uris, Leon 94
Veidt, Conrad 81
Vespucci, Amerigo 16
Viereck, Georg Sylvester 93

Villard, Henry 59
Villard, Oswald Garrison 90
Vocke, Wilhelm 47
Vonnegut, Kurt 94, 104
Wagener, J. A. 47
Wagner 75
Wagner, Robert 85
Wagner, Webster 59
Waldseemüller, Martin 15
Wallers, Major 49
Walter, Bruno 74
Walter, Thomas 79
Wanamaker, John 60
Ward, Robert E. .... ix, 93, 139
Washington 39, 41
Weber 60, 75
Weber, Paula 94
Weitzel, Major-General 45
Welsbach 60
Welsers 16
Wenders, Wim 82
Werner, Oscar 81
White, Andrew 69
Whitman 94
Whittier 94
Wilder, Billy 81
Wilhelm, Prinz of Zweibrücken 40
Willich, Major-General 45, 46
Wilson, President 119
Wistar, Caspar 57
Wurlitzer, Franz Rudolph 60

Wyerhaeuser, Frederick 60
Zenger, Johann Peter 90
Zeppelin, Count 56
Zerrahn, Carl 73
Ziebarth 58
Zimmermann, Eugene 80
Zinnemann, Fred 81
Zuendt, Ernst Anton 93